ADVANCE PRAISE FOR *GET WITH IT, GIRLS!*

"Thanks for sharing Get with It, Girls! *with me. Teri focused on all the right things for girls who aspire to be successful as athletes."*
— Val Ackerman, WNBA president

"Now I see how she was beating us all these years."
— Larry Bock, volleyball coach, Juniata College

"Having never been a girl myself, I found Teri's book loaded with valuable information. I've had three daughters involved with athletics. I went through the book with my 14-year-old and she really enjoyed it. The anecdotes. The stories. The advice. It was a wonderful illustration for her on how to handle certain situations. And it was a resource manual for me on how to approach the everyday relationship that a father has with a daughter, especially one who participates in sports. But anybody who has children, not just daughters, would find this an excellent read."
— Dan Dierdorf, NFL Hall of Fame, CBS broadcaster

"I love the book. There is so much great stuff here — for life, not just for sports. I was overwhelmed at the amount of information. My daughter and I had lively discussions on some topics, not disagreeing with Teri, just working them out. I would have loved to have this book to back me up when my girls were young. I want to hand this out to some educators. If I were teaching teenage girls right now, I would put this in use immediately."
— Terry Edelmann, community relations director, St. Louis Catholic Education Office

"I think your book is fabulous. It does a terrific job of blending everyday examples of sports and the abstract lessons we can get out of them. At no time does the tone seem

to preach. It feels like a good conversation between two people. I enjoyed the emphasis on being a well-rounded person. All kids should hear that life is more than just being an athlete. Your focus on being pro-active in order to achieve goals is a great one."
— Kristin Folkl, forward, WNBA Minnesota Lynx

"I looked at the book both as a mother and as a mother of a daughter who is a 15-year-old athlete. It's just good sound principles, like self-discipline, that all girls need in order to mold themselves into young ladies. Teri shows how these principles are transferable from competition in sports to other arenas in life. As mothers, we are also coaches in a way. So I just really appreciate what Teri has done . . . although I'm not sure if it's a parental guide to coaching, or a coaching guide to parenting!"
— Mary Elizabeth Grimes-Nutt, executive director,
Elite International Sports Marketing

"Thanks for the chance to read this encouraging book. It was very inspirational to me. I thought of countless applications, not only for my 14-year-old daughter, but for me as well. Teri has really hit the mark with her examples of hard work, discipline, humor, and determination. This is an important work for female athletes to read as they seek to understand competition and themselves. It is now in the hands of my 14-year-old, and I can't wait to discuss it with her."
— Rick Horton, director, Fellowship of Christian Athletes/former pitcher,
St. Louis Cardinals, Chicago White Sox, Los Angeles Dodgers

"This is the best gift book for girls I've ever seen."
— Carol Howe-Veenstra, athletic director, College of St. Benedict

"A great coach uses sport as an educational instrument to teach the lessons of life. Here's one coach who has done that for her teams and is now sharing her wisdom and philosophy on a larger playing field. Coach Clemens makes 'competition' a good word."
—Donna A. Lopiano, Ph.D./executive director, Women's Sports Foundation

"It's awesome. This is something that parents should buy for their daughters and just hand to them, instead of lecturing them. It's a genuine lifestyle book for young women. It makes things so clear but not in a parental way. It's upbeat. It's fun. It's easy to read because of the stories that are interwoven. My daughter, Jenny, who is 19, read the whole book and said, 'Mom, I wish you had given me this when I was a freshman or sophomore in high school. It would have saved me a lot of grief.' I'm wondering now how I can make life easier on my younger daughter, Jamie. Now I know. I'm going to give her Teri's book."

— Susie Mathieu, liason for the National Hockey League and
NHL Players Association at the 1998 Winter Olympics

"For any female who wants to be a winner, this is a must-read. It's not just for athletes. It's a must-read for coaches, too. I was completely motivated. It's one idea after another. I'm in awe of the way you're able to inspire people."

— Jenny McDowell, volleyball coach, Emory University

"There's nothing like it on the market. It's wonderful! It's everything I thought it would be and more. I love the chatty style. I swear, while I'm reading it I feel like Teri is in the chair across from me giving me life's lessons. Tell her that I'm picking up a lot of management tricks for myself. Sometimes I feel like the kid, sometimes like the coach."

— Lynn Oris, Barnes & Noble bookstore manager

"In my 25 years of college coaching I've had the opportunity to listen to and work with many talented coaches. Teri Clemens has an enthusiastic style of motivating her student-athletes to play the game harder and at a higher level than the team they are competing against. She is a master at training them to have confidence in their ability to win."

— Dr. Cecile Reynaud, volleyball coach, Florida State University

"I like the book A LOT. I especially liked the Pat on the Back Award. What a great concept for all of us, especially young women! I have always admired Teri's ability to channel her own drive and determination to others. It's one thing to be successful in your own right, but a whole other level of person can make others successful. She is the ultimate coach."

— Ellen Sherberg, publisher, *St. Louis Business Journal*

"Teri spells out, page after page, that competition and fun are not mutually exclusive. It's such a great and needed message. Teri doesn't try to sell the kids on, 'This is a good thing — take your medicine!' She says, 'Do it to have fun and forge friendships for a lifetime.' I love that message. My absolute favorite part was the very end, when Teri's student-athletes commented on how inspiring it was to play for her. I thought their testimony was very special."

— Patty Viverito, senior associate commissioner, Missouri Valley Conference

"The book is really GREAT! Should be required reading for ALL coaches, especially girls' coaches. Would have been required for my teams — but first for me! Teri has a great knack. This is really what women's (and all) sports are about. I don't think there is a thing I could add. In fact, I found myself making mental notes on how to do quite a few things better, starting tomorrow — even though I don't coach. It's really about how to be a winner in life. Great reading!"

— Sheila Walker, consultant/former director for sports programs, U.S. Olympics Committee

"I got a chance to read the copy of the book. I really liked it. It was straightforward, easy to read and makes sense to high performance athletes and beginners alike."
— Hayley Wickenheiser, 1998 Canadian Olympic hockey silver medalist

"She's got 10 bazillion ways of motivating people."
— Joe Worlund, Teri's assistant at Washington University

GET WITH IT, GIRLS!

GET WITH IT, GIRLS!

LIFE IS COMPETITION

TERI CLEMENS

WITH TOM WHEATLEY

DIAMOND COMMUNICATIONS
An Imprint of the Rowman & Littlefield Publishing Group

Lanham • South Bend • New York • Oxford

GET WITH IT, GIRLS!
LIFE IS COMPETITION

Copyright © 2001 by Teri Clemens with Tom Wheatley

Manufactured in the United States of America

Published by Diamond Communications
An Imprint of the Rowman & Littlefield
Publishing Group
4720 Boston Way
Lanham, Maryland 20706

Distributed by National Book Network

Library of Congress Cataloging-in-Publication Data
Clemens, Teri, 1956-
  Get with it, girls! : Life is competition / Teri Clemens with Tom Wheatley.
      p.   cm.
  ISBN 1-888698-37-3
  1. Young women--Conduct of life. 2. Girls--Conduct of life. 3. Women athletes--Conduct of life. 4. Competition (Psychology) 5. Success. I. Wheatley, Tom, 1951- II. Title.
  HQ1229 .C58 2001
  305.242--dc21

                                                    2001017085

TABLE OF CONTENTS

FOREWORD

By Dr. William H. Danforth
Chancellor Emeritus, Washington University in St. Louis

Teri Clemens is not only a very talented coach, she is a very wonderful human being. She has a loving and supportive family to whom she gives her all. She exemplifies courage and determination and personal drive for success.

She has been an inspiration to her players and her colleagues. She cares about her players as people as well as athletes. She cares about their academics and their personal and career successes.

She is a mentor's mentor, a role model's role model. I loved watching her teams. They were different. They were better prepared and better disciplined than their opponents. And they had more fun.

While other teams might look uptight and sometimes angry with themselves or with the coach, Teri's teams laughed and encouraged one another. I have never seen groups more mutually supportive. All teams have ups and downs, but I never saw one of her teams fall apart.

Seeing a group of people perform as they did was like watching magic happen in the real world. To me, she is not only a role model's role model, she is also a leader's leader.

She can change your life.

With my mentor, Dr. William H. Danforth.

"In this world of give and take, there are few who are willing to give what it takes."
—Anonymous

To those few...

HERE'S THE DEAL
(INTRODUCTION)

"Competition is my calling card."

You may already think you're a strong competitor. I'm writing to encourage you to upgrade that level, whether you're a rookie or advanced in the game. Some believe that our competitive level is already determined at birth. I think not. God gave us the makeup and the guidance. We make ourselves the competitors that we are.

There are specific skills that determine our competitive ability. Just like getting in shape for a sport, we need to be conditioned to become better competitors. In athletics, we might train in distance running or plyometrics or weight lifting. In training for competition, the skills include confidence, self-esteem, passion, and fun, among others.

Having fun's a skill? Absolutely! In my book, it is. Read on. Humor helps us work through things more quickly. When we take things too seriously, it's difficult to relax. It makes us tight. When we laugh, our minds open up. And we perform better. Humor attaches us to the people we're laughing with. It helps to bond a group or a team.

I can't even count how many times that my volleyball teams fell on the floor, rolling in laughter. Note that we laughed with each other, not at each other. Light-heartedness creates a special magic. It's contagious.

Training with me will be fun. I'll share lots of stories about players who have developed these skills to a tremendous level. Some of them started out very shy and scared. Some started at elite levels and found they still had room to grow. This book will help those of you who aren't competitive and want to find out if there's some magical level. And it will also help those of you who already have the magic, but want to learn advanced tricks!

I remember as a youth not being challenged enough. The emphasis was given to the middle of the team and the middle of the class. What I saw, as a young girl, was the average becoming better and the best becoming complacent.

Teasing the two Jennifers — Cofazza (left) and Martz.

"Humor attaches us to the people we're laughing with."

So I won't neglect the beginner, but I won't neglect the elite performer, either. This book is for everyone. I'll help you find the tools you need to be more competitive. Not just in athletics, but in life. I'll coach you to be as comfortable competing as you are when you're listening to a CD or yakking with a friend on the phone.

I love coaching the skills of competition. I've trained competitive girls all my life. Every year I'd see girls enter their freshman year in high school or college, thinking they knew what it took to be the best and to reach their dreams. They found that there was always room to grow. And then we'd grow together.

Here's who I am. I love to be challenged. I love to laugh, but I'm not afraid to cry. And clearly, I'm the most competitive person I know! I consider it my very best trait. And I consider it my very worst trait. There's a balance you have to have, and that's not always easy to achieve.

There's no doubt that in my own athletic experience, I'd give everything it takes to be the best. If a coach told me to get eight hours sleep, I'd get 10. If my tennis coach told me to hit 100 ground strokes a day, I'd hit 200. And I'd do it in the morning and again in the afternoon. If my teacher told me to write a five-page essay, I'd write 10.

So I'm writing this book for all girls, including me. I intend to use it as my handbook and my reminder, too. I've never compiled all my thoughts on competitiveness in one place. I've been too busy competing.

In my back pocket, I carry a lot of history. As a college athlete, I won most valuable player awards in three sports. As a volleyball coach, my high school teams won three state titles in six years. In 14 years as head volleyball coach at Washington University, we won seven national titles, six of them in a row. Because of Washington University's commitment and trust in me, I was able to leave coaching with the highest winning percentage in collegiate history.

I'm only sharing this so you can see where I'm coming from. When you win a championship, there is a special feeling. All winners know that. Listening to the winners in this book will jumpstart you.

I've never been big on long speeches. If people want to play volleyball, they put up a net. If people want to play the piano, they bang the keys. If people want to be more competitive, they may already be reading Chapter 6.

So turn the page and get going, girls!

WHY COMPETE?
(PREPARE TO WIN)

*"The only reason to play the game is so we know
what to work on in practice."*

It was a tough moment. My daughter Manda was six years old and always hung around the gym with me. One day she looked up and said, "Mom, what's a tomboy?" I was almost embarrassed for my generation. I said, "A tomboy is what some used to call a girl who competes in sports." And Manda said, "Well, what do they call a boy, a jennygirl?"

Manda wasn't trying to be funny. It never crossed her mind that sports were once reserved for boys. What her innocence showed was that girls have arrived. Boys play sports. Girls play sports.

Competition is healthy — in all facets of life. And it will happen whether we like it or not. So you better get used to it. Competing includes constantly being pushed down and finding ways to get back up.

Are you born to be a competitor? Well, you might be born with that makeup,

1

"Start thinking like a winner. You'll start, carrying yourself differently. You'll start seeing things differently. You'll be different."

Carly Clemens, age 5, winner in training.

but you can also definitely learn to compete. Even though I always craved competition from an early age, I still look for ways to improve on a daily basis.

My sister Sherri used to say that I was competitive in my sleep. We used to compete at night with the lights out in our bedroom, trying to see how long we could talk before our dad caught us. We knew he was coming when we heard the coins jingling in his pocket as he walked down the hall. And then we'd pretend to be asleep when he came in.

It was a silly kind of competition, but competition just the same. In sports, and in life, it's not just about winning the big game or acing the big test. Life throws us countless little challenges every day. At the Clemens home, competition is a way of life for me, my husband, our four daughters, and our two sons. We thrive on it. We prepare for it. And the competitiveness — oh, my gosh, it's unbelievable. Every day there is a driveway basketball game or a race to finish the daily chores. It's certainly a lively home, with lots of encouragement and pats on the back. So, of course Manda thinks that sports are for everyone. It's all she knows.

And competition isn't drudgery at our house. It's fun. It's life. The same was true in the Washington University volleyball gym. It was the practices that I loved, much more so than the games. The game is just an evaluation to see where we are. The game is the test. The key is the practice, the preparation, not the game. The key is what you do all week, what you do everyday in life. That's what's really important, not the test itself.

A job interview is a great example. You can't just judge your life by how you do in that interview. It's just a test, a test to see where you are at that time. Am

I ready to take this position? Am I confident? Am I presenting myself well? It's just a test. We find out what we need to go back and work on.

I saw my players, as college seniors, interview for jobs. I watched their confidence grow as they attended more and more interviews. They didn't fear rejection. They enjoyed the challenge. Competitors take risks, and risk-taking is not always safe or comfortable. But it is necessary to get better, to get stronger, to be a winner.

There are times when you will struggle. Look at me. As a coach, I lived a life where competition was a glaring daily focus. Every time I looked up, there was a scoreboard in my face, telling me if I was ahead. I relished it. But I couldn't possibly define my life by that scoreboard. *I* decide that I am a winner—not the scoreboard.

It's still true in my life today. As a competitor, there are factors that will slow me down or change my direction. That's what I'm facing now. I had to retire from coaching. In the last few years, my simple case of asthma became life-threatening with severe complications. Coaching was everything for me, but not at the risk of my health and quality time with my family. As a competitor, I didn't want to give in to the illness. As a winner, I had to make smart choices.

If I had an asthma attack while driving to practice, I knew I could make a right turn to the hospital or a left turn to the gym. The decision should have been obvious. I made the wrong choice many times before I figured it out — proof that competitors *can* get it right. I had to leave coaching. It was the hardest choice I've ever made. My lungs may be sick, but it's my heart that is broken. It aches every day. But a winner finds new challenges. And I have.

We choose to make life fair or unfair. It doesn't just happen. It's not realistic to think it should always be fair. Don't expect life to be perfect. Go with it.

What if you don't get a date for the prom? You didn't do anything wrong, but things didn't work out the way you wanted. It doesn't seem fair. Kids really like that word: "Fair." When I was little, my brother and I often would share an ice cream sandwich. If he broke it in two and handed me the smaller piece, it was easy for me to yell, "Hey, that's not fair." If I got to pick first, I wasn't complaining. Now it was fair. Sometimes life *seems* very unfair.

So you didn't get a date for the prom, and you think life isn't fair. But the girl who got the date you wanted thinks life is *really* fair! Or your teacher grades the exam on a curve, and you're at the bottom and think it's unfair. But the girl at the top loves the curve.

That's why I say: "Get with it, girls! Don't focus on whether something's fair or unfair. Just get the job done." One of my players, Brielle Killip, understood that better than most.

We did not recruit her. We had a great team coming back, and we had already recruited a great rookie class. I really didn't need another player. But KC — we called her that because she's from Kansas City — persistently wrote me letters all summer. She also sent me her own highlight video. I finally responded with, "Well, you can come out and walk on." We were not going to make it easy, and there were no guarantees. We had walk-ons make the team before, but none had made it through the program for all four years.

We told KC to come to campus early. We didn't invite her to the team meeting or the team picture. She and six other walk-ons had a tryout with my assistant coach, Joe Worlund, at 7 AM on the first day of practice. The others did not make it, but Joe kept KC and drilled her alone for 30 more minutes. That's a grind when you're going solo. There's no time to rest. Her family came with her from Kansas City, and her parents were taking pictures of her through this little window across from the gym.

They were excited that she even had a tryout with a college team. It was obvious that this family really cared and treasured the moment. And KC played well.

Joe was really impressed. He told me that she had spunk. I thought, "Really? Her family has spunk, too." So we arranged for her to try out right then with me. And then I just drilled her for another half hour. It was grueling. I wanted to see if she had staying power. She definitely did. I kept a tough outward appearance, but I was grinning inside. She was my kind of player. But we still did not commit to her yet. Next, the whole team was going on a four-mile run. We told her she could join them. And she finished in the top half — after an hour of one-on-one workouts!

Then I invited her to the 9 AM workout for rookies only. She was still trying out. We still had not committed, although we already knew we wanted her. No matter what we threw at her, it motivated her more.

The challenge turned her on. The rookies practiced for another hour, and with just six people it was tough. She went through all this and was a real teamer. She was vocal. She was highly spirited. She had started working out long before the other rookies, and *she* was encouraging them.

We started calling her KC right then. Brielle was just too soft for how she was playing. And it's too bad, because Brielle is one of my absolute favorite names! When the rookie workout was over, we gave her a practice jersey and said, "You can borrow this for the first full workout with the whole squad."

So she and the other rookies went through a three-hour practice. When we finally finished that afternoon, I told the team, "That was a great opening to a championship season. Welcome, KC, to the Washington University volleyball team." She had tears, and all the players started hugging her and welcoming her.

It was a no-brainer to take such a competitor. She made us a better team. She started all year as a rookie, and we won the national championship. She was the same kind of competitor in academia. She studied graphic design, and when she put her portfolio together, she couldn't wait for her professor to see it. She couldn't wait to be evaluated. Most kids dread that. It's a grueling day of being judged, just like her first tryout in volleyball. Yet that experience helped her prepare for the portfolio test.

KC's volleyball career is over now, but she's forever a competitor. I can't imagine any day that will be too tough for her. She is able to look on the bright side, because she is always prepared. And when you're prepared, you invite competition. Her championship ring stands as such a symbol of her competitiveness.

So prepare like KC. Start thinking like a winner. You'll start carrying yourself differently. You start seeing things differently. You'll be different.

Forget the tomboy label. You're a winner.

"Passion creates magic"

Intensity in triplicate: All-America players Lisa Becker (left), Joanie Subar (right), and Anne Quenette (backcourt). (Washington University in St. Louis Photographic Services)

WHAT TURNS YOU ON?
(FIND YOUR PASSION)

"Anything you love doing is not work, no matter how much you sweat."

Oh, I have passion. An incredible passion. A deep love for something. I want it with all my heart, with all my soul. I crave it. I dream about it. It gives me goose bumps. I don't even care if it's raining outside. I'm singing in the shower 'cause I've got it. It's volleyball. That's my passion. What's yours?

You're trying to decide: What do I want to do? What do I want to be? What's important to me? And sometimes you have several areas of passion. And that's awesome. They can also be short-lived or long-term. They can remain constant or ever changing. And age is not a factor.

My daughter Carly, at age nine, just came back from her first day ever at basketball camp. When her dad picked her up afterward, she ran into his arms and screamed, "Dad, it was so much fun! And they said tomorrow will be even more fun!" There you have it. That was the start of a new passion.

In grade school, I had two huge passions. Sports and music. My parents encouraged both. It was good to have them on my side. I got up every morning with my brother Larry, sister Sherri, and two friends and sang at the 5:30 church service before school. I did that five days a week for four years. In the summer, the service was at 7 AM, so we got to sleep in! A lot of times there was nobody attending the service — except for the five of us. Isn't that sad? But we didn't care! We were really passionate about it. We weren't doing it for an audience. The five of us loved it. I don't even remember who started our choir, but I remember that my parents were so proud of us. That's part of why we compete, too — for the pride we have in ourselves and that others have in us.

My first sports passion was softball. Larry and I threw every day in the street in front of our house. He threw so hard that my hand ached. I never admitted that to him, but I remember that my mom secretly stuck a sponge in my glove to ease the sting. Without even saying a word, she supported my passion and helped me improve. So while I'm thinking about it, Mom, thanks!

Developing a passion is sometimes done by watching others. These people are your role models. I had a number of them. Still do. Sister Marlene, who taught me how to play guitar. Coach Adams, who inspired me to coach. And Dr. Danforth at Washington University, who is a favorite mentor.

I'm a role model myself, and I take it very seriously. I know that young girls watch me. How I present myself. What I have to say. My values. My sense of humor. My passion. I'm so honored now that the players I coached are influencing other young girls. It goes on and on and on. The same passions we shared, they're now sharing with others.

One of my players, Christine Masel, found her passion for coaching later than I did. After she graduated, she was an engineer in Dallas, and she was making excellent money. One day she called me up and said, "Coach, you're going to think this is really wacko, but I just know in my heart I want to be a volleyball coach." That same afternoon, the athletic director from Christian Brothers College in Memphis happened to call me for advice in filling their volleyball vacancy.

I said, "Are you willing to take a chance on a novice?" The answer was yes, and "Mase" had a new career. A year later, she took the head coaching position at the University of Chicago, in our conference, and coached against me. This was a difficult challenge for her. But her heart is beating stronger because she has passion back in her life.

That same passion was obvious when Mase played for me. Once we had a showdown with the number-one team, the University of California-San Diego, on their court. Packed house. Band blaring. Road fans louder than we'd ever heard. We trailed two games to nothing, in a best-of-five format. We won the third game quickly, but we were down 12-14 in the fourth game. Every single time San Diego served, the announcer yelled, "Maaaaaaatch point!" The entire crowd would stand up. Then we would come up with some great play and hold them off. And they'd all sit down again.

That happened 10 times. The 10th time, Mase — who, believe me, was not known at all for her defense — made one of the most unbelievable, scoop-the-ball-out-of-the-bleachers-backward-over-the-head saves I've ever seen. And we went on to win the game and the match — *the* match of my coaching career. No surprise that Mase's passion for volleyball is still alive and burning.

Announcing that you have a passion will not make victories fall in your lap. You have to work at it. My players put in an enormous amount of hours. This commitment was not always obvious to others, because they only saw the end result. Our work ethic was unmatched.

Take Amy Albers and Liz Jokerst, two girls from two small towns who never met until they walked into our gym. Amy — or Al, as we called her — was a superstar, two-time national player of the year, three-time All-America middle blocker, probably the best player in Division III history. Liz was a role player. They both gave the same amount to the program, but a special part of Liz's contribution was invisible to the naked eye. She was unbelievably dedicated to off-season weight-lifting. That was Al's least favorite part of our program. Liz's enthusiasm for muscle definition inspired all of us. She took it upon herself to push Al into the weight room with her. We were all better because of it.

So while I'm thinking about it, Liz, thanks to you, too! You showed us that passion expresses itself in different ways. You gave selflessly, without publicity. Don't think we didn't notice!

Passion creates magic. It happens when we pour our heart and soul into what we do. Each of us has power within us. What we're looking for is flow, to be in almost a trance-like state where any move we make is successful. We perform so fluidly that our actions seem effortless. It's happened to me oftentimes in sports, in music, even in my cross-stitch. It's a powerful feeling. You'll know when you get there. Your package will seem complete.

People ask, "Why did you keep coaching after you won a national championship?" Because once we reached that state of flow, I wanted it for my players again and again and again. And that flow affects everything else in life. I want that same feeling in everything I do.

Success in any passion demands stick-to-it-iveness. How do we get that? Education is key. If you keep studying your craft, you will become more knowledgeable. And that will keep motivating you. It'll keep your passion alive. Persevere, girls. The slips and trips may slow you down, but don't let them consume you.

In the heat of competition, I encourage a good pat on the back between teammates. I love that. It's a great way to celebrate happy moments. The encouragement better not come because a player is sulking, pouting, or whining. That would be forced, as though she were asking for attention. She and her teammates should move forward and focus on the next play. So when you're frustrated, try not to ask — by word or body language — for a pat on the back. I've done it. You've done it. But let's not make it a habit. Let's maintain a good emotional level. You'll discover a better flow, especially when you push the limit.

Give everything you've got to your passion. Push the limit. I remember the first day of practice at Washington University for Lisa Becker, who would be named national player of the year as a senior. She knew she had a passion for volleyball. But after sweating through five practice uniforms that first day, she blasted through to a level she never knew existed.

Most of my rookies did the same thing. Push the limit. After that first day, Lisa came up to me and said, "I had no idea it could be like this. I had no idea it could be this good. I can't wait till tomorrow!"

What I found rewarding was that passion could be so contagious. The friend-ships. The lessons. The sweat. The laughter. The intensity. The emotion. The strength. The spirit. The courage. The determination.

That's what passion is all about. Push the limit!

WINNERS OR WHINERS
(SUCK IT UP)

"Winners are winners long before the trophies are given out."

I prefer to define a winner by her work ethic, rather than by her awards. Measure the drive of your passion, not the result. What's important is the climb. It's not necessarily who wins the last game of the season. It's not necessarily who gets the biggest part in the school play or whose painting wins the art fair.

The actual winning is the process of competing at your best. Of course we keep score. You want to know when the game ends! Don't get me wrong, I want my team's name on top. But there's much more to it than that. Some people have the wrong idea about who's a winner and who's not.

Winners give strong effort, day in and day out. I constantly expected my players to have a grittier work ethic than the opposition. Then my expectations became their expectations.

Winners do not have lame excuses. That's what differentiates them from

"Winners are confident enough in their own position, and in their own person, to share. At some point you realize that everything you give to others comes back to you."

Teammates Shelley Swan (left) and Claire Zellers share a light-hearted moment on court. (Washington University in St. Louis Photographic Services) whiners. They are not too tired. They are not too sore. They are not too weak.

Our personalities are not what define us as strong or weak. It doesn't matter if I'm introverted or extroverted. Quiet doesn't mean weak, and loud doesn't mean strong. When we built our teams, some players were boisterous and others were extremely shy. I did not discount either personality from being a winner. What counts is having that great attitude, that passion and drive.

When I first started coaching at Washington University, Lori Nishikawa was my first recruit. She came to visit the campus with her mom, and I don't think Lori spoke that entire weekend. In fact, I don't think she spoke her whole first year! But I wasn't worried about her communicating. When she got a volleyball in her hands, she showed poise, leadership, and talent. She communicated through competition.

Lori was never outgoing the whole four years she played for me. Despite her shyness, she was my starting setter as a rookie. We won our first national championship in her senior year. And she was a two-time national player of the year. She wasn't a rah-rah player. It may be important to have a rah-rah player out there, but it wasn't within her to be that. She was comfortable with herself. I loved that.

Lori did learn that there were times when she had to speak up. Being shy did not excuse her from sharing specific information while competing. Sometimes you *must* talk. There were times when I yanked her out of a drill and said, "That is unacceptable. You are running the offense. You must call the plays." This had nothing to do with her shy personality. Sometimes you just have to leave your comfort zone.

Winners also like to share their strengths with other people. As a coach, I was constantly asked about our secrets. What made us so close-knit? How were we able to laugh on the court and still win? Why were we obviously such great friends? So when I spoke at coaching clinics, I unabashedly shared how we did it. And then people asked: "How can you give away the secrets of your success?"

Easy. The other coaches aren't me, and I'm not them. They couldn't beat me just because I clued them in. It would take more than that. They have different players with different personalities and different skills. And we all communicate differently. So when I coach other coaches, I just never see it as a threat.

And my players were the same way with each other. When they found something that worked for them, on or off the court, they shared it with their teammates. Winners don't worry that others might improve enough to move ahead of them. You're playing the role of a winning teammate. Winners are confident enough in their own position, and in their own person, to share. At some point you realize that everything you give to others comes back to you.

It's the whiner who says, "I'm not helping her. I want to beat her out." Winners don't stress their own individual success. When our players made an all-tournament team, we saw it as a reward for the team. We all contributed. Individual player awards found a home in my office until the end of each season. Then the players quietly came and got them. Winners don't need medals hanging around their necks. They share them with teammates.

Kristin Folkl, a forward with the Minnesota Lynx of the WNBA, is a great example. When she was in high school in St. Louis, she helped St. Joseph Academy win four state titles in volleyball and four in basketball. She won the Dial

Award as the top female high school athlete in America. At Stanford University, she helped win three national volleyball titles and also played in the basketball Final Four twice.

Kristin was on my volleyball team at the 1994 U.S. Olympic Festival. Through tons of interviews, Kristin constantly gave credit to her teammates. Classy. And smart. I always told my players that when they had an interview or were caught in a clumsy conversation, "Give credit, especially when you're nervous." Always keep that in your back pocket. If you can't think of anything to say, which is often a big fear, just give credit to others. It's so easy. It's what winners do.

My players learned to do that, and they told me it saved them many a time. And it's saved me, too. It works beautifully in a team situation. If a reporter asks, "Aren't you proud of that last hit?" you could say, "Meg set a beautiful ball for me." You've made yourself feel proud. And when the person you're praising hears it, she'll also feel proud. You deflected credit to her and gave her greater value. That's what a winner does. Never be critical. That's what a whiner does. That's in the spirit of ugliness.

Girls really have to learn: It's okay to critique, it's not okay to be critical. We addressed that very early every season. And it's something that girls don't always want to hear. I'm being critical if I say, "That set stunk. Set the ball higher." It's not being critical if I say, "Can you set the ball a little higher?" That's critiquing. And that's positive. That's how we improve. There is nothing mean being said there at all. If I get a better ball to hit, that will make us a better team. And that's what we want.

"Us girls" need to get over that. Critiquing helps us improve. That's a winning style. It's okay to ask Abby, "Can you pick me up a little early today for practice?" You don't want to say, "You're always late, so pick me up early." Then Abby will run to Mary and say, "Can you believe her? She told me not to be late!"

The whiner takes the cheap shot and tries to show she's better, or smarter, than the other person. I have to watch myself, because the smart-aleck comments come easy to me. But I try to work hard to avoid negative and hurtful comments. And if I do slip, and sometimes I do, I apologize and move on.

That's another point for winners. If you have a problem with someone, address it with that person. Whiners are impulsively critical. They backstab, too. Winners go directly to the source. That approach will help us in every facet of life. We won't gossip as much. We all slip here and there. Just don't be critical. Don't be ugly. Every once in a while, step back and evaluate your behavior. And admit when you've gone overboard.

I have stopped many, many a practice to say to a player, "There's a better way to say that." Winners critique. Whiners criticize. I can't emphasize that enough.

I don't spend much time differentiating between girls and guys as athletes. But there is a key difference that can keep females from being winners. I know this is a generalization, but it's valid. Guys can play guys across a volleyball net and be highly competitive. They can yell at each other and go after each other hard. Then they can still walk out of the gym as buddies and ask each other, "Where should we eat tonight?"

In the same situation, with 12 girls instead of 12 guys, they can yell at each other and go after each other hard. And when the workout is over, instead of putting their arms around each other and saying, "Where should we eat to-night," Melissa will throw her arms around Melanie and say, "I'm never talking to Monica again after what she did."

The emotions of girls are wonderful, but I think there's something to be learned from both genders here. Again, it's a generalization, but it does happen. In our gym, whenever that piddly stuff crept in, we stamped it out. We went hard at each other every day at practice and remained buddies. And we knew we had something special.

Actions also separate winners from whiners. Remember the World Cup win for the American women soccer team? Simply amazing. As inspired as I was with the victory, one moment disappointed me. The player who scored the winning goal in the shootout ran down the field by herself, took her shirt off and waved it. The whole nation celebrated, but part of me was crushed. I wondered, "What's she doing? What's going on here? Does she have an endorsement deal for sports bras or what?"

I may be the only person in America who sees it that way. But her teammates were all running toward her, and she ran off by herself as if to say, "Look at me!" She may have scored the last goal in the overtime shootout. But what about her teammates who scored the first, second, third, and fourth goals in overtime? And the incredible save by the American goalie to set the stage?

A winner's first thoughts should have been to run to the huddle, to run to her teammates, to share the championship. You have to develop an awareness of that. *You have to decide ahead of time to react like a winner*. Otherwise, the emotion of the moment might overwhelm you. Remember what we said: "Just because you have the higher score at the end of the game doesn't make you a winner. Winning involves the whole package of behaviors."

Hey, we won seven national championships, and I don't even remember who got the last point in any of them. After each victory, our whole team celebrated together. Everyone just piled on top of each other at the middle of the court. Why would it be any other way? We worked tirelessly together to get to that moment. We couldn't imagine celebrating any other way.

It was the intensity of our work ethic that culminated in a magical celebration. Each individual had to work hard to produce our kind of success. Even though we had superstars, no one was above the daily grind of practice. It wasn't enough just to beat opponents. We wanted to outwork them, no matter what their talent level.

The point is, winners work toward their goals, giving everything they have to improve each day they compete. They cannot give a cheap effort, even though it might be enough to win the game. Whiners are satisfied to win by just one point, not necessarily pushing themselves to their limit. Winners have their own agenda.

The nature of many people is to embrace the underdog and dislike winners. The truth is, it was hard to dislike my teams, because we presented ourselves with class and sportsmanship. And many teams complimented us on that, even after we beat them. Why? We didn't emphasize our *winning*. We emphasized our *working*. And people like workers.

The overall theme of our program was always the same. It's something that my high school coach, Linda Adams, treasured and passed on to me:

"In this world of give and take, there are few who are willing to give what it takes."

Winners give. Whiners take.

DECLARE YOUR INDEPENDENCE
(TAKE CHARGE OF YOURSELF)

"Your life is your life."

As a coach at Washington University, I told each prospect, "When you graduate from this program, you will be an independent young woman." That was important to me because I see myself as someone who is strong enough to think and act for herself.

One of my favorite stories is about one of my players, Nikki "Riz" Gitlin. I was recruiting her in the spring of her senior year of high school. She came for a visit and was sitting in my office with her father. I said to her, "I pride myself in helping my players become independent young women."

She kind of nodded. And I asked, "Are you independent?" And she said, "Oh, yeah, I'm independent . . . Well, I think I'm independent . . . Dad, am I independent?" Her dad didn't say a word. None us did. We all just started to laugh.

23

"You'll be a better competitor if your heart and your mind are making your own decisions."

Nikki "Riz" Gitlin, All-America hitter, takes charge at the net.

Why is this important?

You will be a better competitor if your own heart and your own mind are making your own decisions. If you think about choosing a mate, for example, it's important that you choose someone because you *want* to be with someone — not because you *need* to be with someone. I can look at so many examples of people who are together just because they depend on each other. They're afraid to be out on their own. Isn't that true? My husband Tom and I have been married 20 years and treasure our friendship. We choose to be together. We expect the relationship to grow, to change, to prosper. And we appreciate each other. We don't need to be together. We want to be together.

If you practice independence, you will be comfortable with yourself. And then you become a stronger person. And many women for so long in our society have not practiced independence.

It's the same way with friends. Do you choose a friend because you really want to be with her? Or do you need to be with that friend? I try to choose my friends because they have qualities that make me a happier person or a better person or just allow me to be me when I'm around them. I want to be with them. Sometimes I'm tempted to choose friends for the wrong reasons. Maybe they are in the popular clique, and I crave that connection. Somewhere along the line, I always realize that I'm not one of them. And I don't need to be one of them.

I wish we didn't have to experience that. But we all do. It can be a lesson that just kicks you across the room. Sometimes it hurts. I can't make you safe from that. But I am encouraging you to get back up when you do get kicked around.

People regularly comment about the independence of own six children: Terri

Renee, Will, Eliott, Manda, Carly, and Gabi. At age six, Carly was a free spirit in class and sometimes difficult to keep under control. But her teacher also told me that other students all looked to Carly for advice. What the teacher was telling me was that Carly is a leader, that she's independent, that she has a sense of who she is.

We all have to learn how to keep our independence under control. Carly shouldn't be disrupting things in class. But we don't want to stifle that enthusiasm in her. We want her to learn how to use strengths in a positive way.

So on the outside I'm looking like a concerned parent, because I don't want her to be a problem in class. But on the inside I'm bursting with joy, because my child is independent and a good leader and has great spirit. Those are characteristics I love in a competitor.

We have the ability to choose independence. Start with small steps. Be responsible for your own needs. That's probably how I influenced athletes in what I did as a coach. I treasured watching each player develop independence. I really enjoyed their growth.

And I learned from watching their development, and not just on the volleyball court. I watched them choose careers. And change their minds about 20 times. And come back to maybe what they started with. It's an evolving process and one that may take forever. I like that.

But I always wondered: Are we independent because we're confident? Or are we confident because we're independent? Does it matter? I just know that we need both.

Self-confidence is having the strength to present your ideas: What movie would we want to see? The person with self-worth will think that her choice has value: The movie I want to see is important. That's self-worth.

And then you have to have the confidence to say to somebody else that you want to go see it. And that leads to independence.

Independent people have an opinion. They're not afraid to say it. That's confidence. And they believe their opinion is good. That's self-worth.

But independent people also have the confidence to shut up at times. Sometimes I love when my husband decides what we have for dinner that night. When he chooses, never does it enter my mind that I'm not confident or independent. Sometimes I just don't want to choose. Life combines a lot of opportunities for competition. You choose how to compete, what's important and what isn't.

You don't want to beat a red light or knock people over to be first in the checkout line. One time, my son, Eliott, and my husband were stuck in a long grocery line. A guy about 80 pounds heavier than my husband was in the line in front of them. And Eliott, who was only four years old, said, "Dad, you could you take him out, couldn't you? I think you could beat that guy up." Eliott was eyeing it up. And my husband said, "Well, I might be able to. But not in the grocery store."

How do you become independent?

For some people, it starts with a very small task. It might just be determining that you will phone a friend to go to a movie. Maybe you've never had the confidence to do that, because you're afraid that nobody will go with you. Just take the step. Muster up enough courage to do it. Pick up the phone and make the call. That's how it starts. You decide — because you're reading this chapter or for whatever reason — that you must take one small step. This is the way to change a habit, which leads to an independent lifestyle.

For Riz Gitlin, it was taking many, many small steps. Even though she was brilliant, she still needed direction in college. She had to learn how to study. She had so much energy that it was difficult for her to sit down and get a task done in the classroom.

We knew she had the makings of a good student. But she had to take the initiative to take the first step. It's sounds simple, but it can be hard at first. I know a lot of you don't like to make that first call to a friend, to take that first step.

My son Will, at age 13, would never make that call on his own to a friend. But when I said, "Why don't you phone Jeff and see if he wants to go ride bikes," he said, "Hey, mom, great idea!" He wanted to go, but he wanted no part of initiating a plan. With a little encouragement, he did it. So for him, a huge step toward independence was dialing the phone.

 By the way, that's what coaching is all about. Encouraging, coaxing, demanding. Parents serve that role for you sometimes. Friends can serve that role. We will always need some coaching in our lives. It's the phone call to mom or the hug from a friend. Just someone to give us a little boost.

Every day at our summer volleyball camp, we actually gave out "Patontheback Awards." It's for special performances or extra effort. When we called their names, the girls came up and literally got a pat on the back from every coach, plus a certificate with my handprint on it. My real hope was that the other 175 girls were then motivated to pump up their efforts the next day. Their true reward is that feeling inside when you choose to step it up and step away from the crowd.

That feeling, that intangible sign of independence, is better than a piece of paper. It can never be taken away.

Everyone who shoots for independence will suffer disappointments. Can't help it. Can't control every factor in the world. Independent people probably have more setbacks — and don't call them failures —than those who are dependent. If you take a risk, you can get hurt. If you don't take the risk, you're safer. But you don't grow. You don't move forward. Competitive, independent girls, like Riz, take risks.

Back to that movie you want to see. If you have to call 10 friends till someone wants to go with you, do you call that nine failures? No, it's one success story! The better you get at being independent, the less you even notice when things go against you. It bothers you less. Your attitude gets better. It gets stronger.

One of my volleyball campers named Carrie was also a figure skater. One day she came back from the rink all excited. She told her mom, "Guess what? I almost landed 10 double-loops today!" Her mom said, "Wow, how many did you land?" And Carrie said, "None. But I almost landed 10 of them!" What a great outlook for all of us. Well said, Carrie!

When nine kids say no when you call them to see a movie, you don't think about them. You think about that 10th kid who said yes, and you look forward to the fun ahead.

Whatever we try to achieve, when we finally get there, the key is to forget if we missed it nine or 99 times. If you look at the stories of successful people, they're almost all like that. When Mark McGwire hit his 70th home run to break the big-league record, I'll bet he didn't think about all his strikeouts as he touched homeplate. It was time for celebration.

That's what I note with successful people. They make independent decisions. They make the mistakes but don't dwell on them. And they don't worry what others think about them.

It's all about driving toward competitiveness. If you are independent, you can contribute to individual and team success. If I can call a buddy up on the phone, maybe I have the confidence now to take a piano lesson. Or to try out for a team. The joy of success is much better than the risk of failure.

I don't want to depend on anybody for my success or my failure. It's like ownership for everything I do well in life. And, okay, it's also ownership for everything I do poorly in life. It also comes with laughing at myself. Humor is a necessary tool.

Remember the first day that Riz sat in my office with her dad? Four years later, when she was a senior in college, I was tickled that she had become quite independent. I don't pretend to take full credit for it. It was a team success, not meaning just our volleyball team. She had strong parents at home and strong mentors at Washington University.

Right before her graduation, I smiled and asked Riz, "Are you independent?" She just smiled back at me. She was beaming with pride and confidence. We had never talked about that first day in my office, but it was never to be forgotten. It was clear, it was screamingly clear, that she did not have to run that question past her dad again.

Now she has a position with the National Basketball Association in New York City. That unsure girl has turned herself into an independent young woman.

FUNDAMENTALS FOR LIFE
(EVERYDAY SURVIVAL TIPS)

"You won't find all your ABCs written on the blackboard."

I'm often asked what the magic was in my program. My assistant Joe and I joked that maybe the most obvious secret was hidden right under everyone's noses. What was it? The way we presented ourselves as champions. We insisted that we be champions in life as well as champions in athletics. We never spent the first team meeting of the year talking about X's and O's. We talked about social graces, helping our players feel comfortable in everyday life, with both familiar and unfamiliar situations.

I didn't want my players to have to think about these basic skills of life. I wanted them to be habit forming. It would help them be a better competitor. Period. I wanted them to be comfortable in what sometimes seem to be uncomfortable moments. By learning and practicing these fundamentals of life, you

31

They clean up well! My players looking like winners off the court, too. From left to right:
Diane Vandegrift, Amy Albers, Liz Jokerst, Christine Masel, Amy Sullivan.

"Prepare yourself, girls. Stand tall. Hold your shoulders back. Walk into a room and let your posture make the first statement: 'I've arrived.'"

make others feel good about you. And you feel good about yourself, because you're more at ease with yourself.

As a coach, I wanted my players to react as naturally when shaking the hand of a stranger as they were when passing a volleyball. To pass the ball well, they had to do many repetitions — so many that they could perform that skill in their sleep. In other words, it had to be natural, without thinking. When they did a skill without thinking, we knew that they had mastered it.

If you have to think about how to shake someone's hand, you won't get much accomplished in the conversation to follow. Remember that all the little factors, all the little fundamentals that are required for social skills must also be mastered. My players are champions because they give the same attention to detail in all aspects of their lives.

That's why we addressed these social skills early each season. It's *that* important. Remember, these were young women who came to college at only 17 or 18 years old. Obviously, many of them already had some polished skills. Let's face it, they had to shake my hand to get into the program!

But it's never too late to learn this stuff. I'm telling you to address these fundamentals because you will be a better person. It has nothing to do with trying to impress the public, although it will do that automatically if you practice well. It has to do with being confident in yourself and simply presenting a better you.

No matter what situation occurs, awkward or not, you won't even have to think about what to do. It will just happen. You have practiced your fundamental skills. You will be in control.

Posture is the first key. It's the way that we carry ourselves. Certainly you must have the right posture to perform well in sport, or to play the piano, or to type on a computer. But it's also the first message that you send to other people. It's the first read on us when we walk into a room or present ourselves to someone new.

Good posture sends the message that we like ourselves. It's our introduction. We're presenting ourselves with pride, shoulders back, abdomen tight, head up. When my team walked into a gym, others noticed. We were well-rehearsed. Those in the gym knew that champions had walked in, even in the first tournament of the year.

Some players had good posture when they entered our program. Others needed straightening out! Often it's the girls who grow tall at an early age who are self-conscious. It's so much fun to help them take pride in their stature.

It doesn't matter whether you're tall or short. Or what color your hair is. Or whether you think you're pretty. It's all about promoting the confidence in you. If you're competing in sports, the presentation of yourself to the other team matters. If you're slouching, you look like a wimp. If you stand tall, you're intimidating. You're someone to be reckoned with. If you're making a speech or giving a recital, your presentation to the audience matters. If you slouch, the audience will be nervous with you because they fear a mistake coming their way. If you stand tall, they're confident with you because they feel success coming their way.

Prepare yourself, girls. Stand tall. Hold your shoulders back. Walk into a room and let your posture make the first statement: "I've arrived."

The next fundamental is eye contact. I learned a great lesson when Pope John Paul II held a youth rally in St. Louis. Even near 80 years old and frail, he has learned to conserve his energy for what needs to be communicated. His eyes told me a whole story. Constantly. He could humor a crowd and he could quiet a crowd — just through his eyes. You could see strength in his eyes. You could see spirituality in his eyes.

It reminded me of a drill I actually used to do with myself. I would take a piece of paper and cover up the bottom of my face, below my eyes, and look in a mirror. Then I'd go through a series of expressions to see if my eyes could work a crowd. Could I show shock? Could I show surprise? Could I show concern? And I've never seen anyone with more expressive eyes than Pope John Paul II.

The kids at the rally gave the Pope a hockey stick. He took one little swing. And that one little movement with his hockey stick sent a silent message to that young crowd: "Thank you. I'm with you. I appreciate this gift." It was so simple, and yet the place roared. Such a small gesture brought down a house of 20,000 people. After the Pope did that hockey stick thing, my daughter Gabi, who was just six, was so touched and tickled. She didn't know what he'd been saying up there. But when she saw that, and saw his eyes on the TV, she said, "Mom, he's the goodest man I ever saw." It just reminds us that less is more. His eyes told the story. Eye contact is important — Pope John Paul II eye contact.

I've been in many social situations where I did not have an opportunity to be heard. Now I often give speeches at banquets, but I can think back to my first years as a coach. I was a total peon. I didn't have many wins yet, but I was invited to these dinners because of my position. The only presentation I was able to make then was with my carriage and eyes and smile and handshake. They were all non-verbal communicators, but I could still make a statement.

If you never get to say a word, you can still invite people to know who you are. It's like that whole Cinderella thing. She walked into the ball, carried herself beautifully, all eyes were upon her, and then she left. And she kicked off her little slipper. Without saying a word, she was telling the prince, "Come find me."

It's especially important if you're shy and you don't *want* to say a lot of words. Be expressive. Tell a story with your carriage. And tell a story with your eyes.

Then there is the handshake. Don't underestimate its importance. If anything, overestimate it. The simplest direction I have for any girl is: Always offer *your* hand first. The older generation so often thought that it was proper for the woman to offer her hand first. Whether we think that's true in this politically correct society is not the point. The rules have changed so much that men are confused. So for a girl, always offer your hand first and you're always okay. You'll feel confident, number one. And number two, it makes the person you're greeting feel comfortable, because she/he doesn't have to decide whether to offer the first hand.

Assume you're greeting an older man. Put your right hand out, waist high, fingers forward, thumb up. He will put his hand directly into yours. Then give it one or two firm shakes — and you are done! If you don't want to say anything, just smile. A smile says "I'm happy to meet you" without using words. There, you've done it!

When introduced to someone, always address the person by name. If someone says, "This is Mary," you should say, "Hi, Mary," instead of just "Hi." It personalizes the meeting, which makes the person feel comfortable. By the way, it's the same with apologizing. Instead of just saying "I'm sorry" because your mom *told* you to do so, say, "I'm sorry, Mary." It sends a personal message.

And in an introduction, using the person's name helps you remember it. That's a huge plus. I don't claim to be good with names, but I try to be good with names. By reciting a name aloud, it helps store the name in my memory.

And the next time I meet that person and know the name, I'm proud. When I shake hands, instead of just a smile I'll have the confidence to say, "Hi, Mary." And now we can develop rapport, which is a connection. And that increases both of our comfort zones.

I'm not pretending to be Miss Manners. I don't even want to be. I just want to be so comfortable with the fundamental skills for life that I can use them without thinking. I can enter any new situation now and manage myself, whether I want to be there or not.

Even at a funeral. That's the most uncomfortable place for me. I never want to go, but I always want to pay my respects to the deceased and to the loved ones who are in pain. But it's hard. I'm in this somber place, often with people I don't know. It's a sad occasion, and often there are lots of tears. So prepare. I learned to look at it differently. I try to see it as a celebration of that person's life. I think of our happy moments together. If need be, I can share those thoughts with others at the funeral. I'm more comfortable because I have a plan of action. I also keep in mind that words may not be necessary. Touch is also comforting. A hug may be all that is needed.

Those are the skills for life that my teams tried to master. Just like that volleyball pass, their social skills became second nature. Surprises didn't surprise us.

We were comfortable in uncomfortable situations. We prepared for unforeseen circumstances. We were not worriers. We could always focus on the task at hand. Intriguing how others spent so much time noticing us as we just went about our business.

Now make it your business.

THE COMFORT ZONE
(TAKING RISKS)

"If you're afraid to trip on a crack, get off the sidewalk."

Our comfort zone is where we feel most at ease. To be a winner, to be competitive in life, you have to force yourself to leave your comfort zone sometimes. We talked before about being comfortable with yourself, but you can fall into complacency. You can be too comfortable, which keeps you sitting in the recliner and watching television. The longer you sit in the chair, the more comfortable it is and the less you ever want to get out.

The competitive girl doesn't say, "Oh, there's nothing to do." She evaluates her options, makes a plan and goes. She looks at each day as an opportunity. Leaving your comfort zone helps you to learn more about yourself. Clearly, you must have a certain confidence to take the risk. And since you're gaining in independence, you're also gaining in confidence. You're ready.

If you want to improve, and reach beyond where you are right now, you'll

"My expectations for risk-taking sound simple. I expect you to keep working...keep laughing...keep loving. If you meet these expectations, you can expect to keep winning."

Emmy Sjogren, yet another of my All-America players, gave new meaning to leaving one's comfort zone. (Washington University in St. Louis Photographic Services) likely make yourself slightly uncomfortable before reaching a new comfort level. You can look at it as flights of stairs. Put yourself in the Empire State Building. You feel fine standing there in the lobby. Very comfortable. Until someone challenges you, almost dares you to take the stairs to the top of the building. All 1,860 of them. I, for one, could not say no to that, no matter how painful it sounds. Now we have a goal. To reach the top. Each landing between stairs represents a new comfort zone.

As you climb, you'll discover that while each step gets harder, your drive gets bigger. You become more of a competitor. The muscle-burn is a symbol of pride. When you finish, your prize is ownership. Not of the Empire State Building, but of the victory. You took a risk and now you also own a new comfort level.

In my 20 years of coaching, I never kept a practice outline. And we had some pretty good practices! So that's a lot of planning to throw in the trashcan every night. But I did. That alone forced me to leave my comfort zone every day of my career. I had to start fresh every morning, and that made our practices fresher. Because I took the risk.

How do you know when to leave your comfort zone?

Everything becomes routine. Maybe you're not smiling enough. You're not as eager to perform or to do what it is you're doing. Your friends call and ask you to join them and you say no. If you play the piano, and you're not excited to practice, you're in a rut. You're stuck in a comfort zone. It boils down to this: You need a different challenge. Come on. You know when you need a change. Don't make me coach you on something this obvious.

And competitive people welcome a challenge. They're not afraid of something new or more difficult. They like the challenge to change often, and they like the task to remain tough. Even if that makes them a little uncomfortable at the start. Competitive people like it when there's a real struggle to reach the goal. It may seem impossible at some point, but real competitors don't quit. They just keep going.

My expectations for risk-taking sound simple. I expect you to keep working. I expect you to keep improving. I expect you to keep laughing. And I expect you to keep loving. If you meet these expectations, you can expect to keep winning.

With these expectations come demands. The demands are that we focus, that we drive, that we hustle. I expected all those things from my players. At Washington University, it was a given that these expectations would be met every day. It should be a given in your home, too. Once you accept high expectations, you will be empowered. You'll be a stronger person. I loved it that my players had the same high expectations for me that I had for them, so I couldn't slack off. And I didn't want to — because winners aren't slackers.

The need for risk-taking is inside every one of us. You might not see it clearly at first if you're stuck in a comfort zone. It's safe. It's like home base. But there are no rewards in safety. And success is not just a tangible reward. Being a winner is a feeling. Some girls like to play for the trophies. If you come to my house, you won't see any trophies. I've got dozens of them, but I don't want them in my face. I play for what's intrinsic, what's inside. It's intangible. It's that feeling you get when you challenge yourself to get better. And then you do!

Every season, my team set out to win the national championship. That may sound unreasonable at times, but we planned to win every match, every tournament. I always talked about the feeling. I'm not sure we all had the *same* feeling, but we all talked about it. And when we won our first national championship, or second, or third, or seventh, we all wished the same feeling on our friends and family. It was *that* special. Everyone who's won, who's reached a pinnacle, knows that feeling. And you cannot describe it to others very easily. But that's why it makes me want to encourage all of you. It's worth leaving your comfort zone to get that feeling. Guaranteed.

How do you leave that comfort zone?

That's the beauty of having a coach, a teacher, or a really good buddy. All of us need motivators in our lives. Look at me. I *am* a motivator, and I still need a motivator at times. Not all of us are self-motivated at the same level — but checking out of our comfort zone is something we all can do.

It may mean starting a totally new activity. Or it may mean adding a more challenging level to an activity you're already in. Don't let your peer-pressure groups stop you from taking risks or making changes. They're not going to the same places you are. And never quit asking yourself what you're going to be when you grow up. Whether you're age 10 or 50 or 90, it shows that you're still moving along if you're still asking yourself where you're heading.

It's great to keep changing. I went through — and I'm still going through — a lot of phases. I wanted to be a nurse. Then I wanted to be a top musician. I wanted to be a doctor and a lawyer. I wanted to be everything there is. For me eventually, it was a long-term commitment to coaching. I treasure the title "Coach."

But I'm going to have more titles in life. I might be a politician. I might be a pro golfer, even though the peer pressure from my foursome says no! Right now, I'm thinking I might just climb those 1,860 stairs in the Empire State Building.

Doesn't it excite you to think about all of the possibilities that exist for you? Other people may have their own expectations for you, too. They may not be the same as your expectations for yourself. They may think you're aiming too high or not high enough.

How do you deal with that tension and pressure?

I think of it as being heart-smart. That's the sense of satisfaction inside me. Heart-smart is when I just *know* something is right. You have the same ability. Listen to your heart. When you do something good for someone else and feel good inside, that's heart-smart. You know it is good. You didn't have to share it with anybody. You knew in your heart. That's the same feeling you get when you do something good for yourself.

When I chose to become a coach, I knew I was being heart-smart. But how do you explain that to other people? You don't. Maybe you want to be a lawyer, and others say, "Oh, you only have a 'C' average." Or maybe you have an "A" average and they want you to be a lawyer, but your heart is somewhere else. What makes one person tick doesn't make another person tock.

Other people always have opinions on what you should be doing. Don't just tell them to buzz off. Most people who offer advice really mean well. Don't be offended. I'm tickled that my dad still has advice for me. To this day. Oftentimes on a daily basis! And I'm 44 years old. He still thinks he'll be my caddy when I'm on the pro golf tour. Rather than look at it negatively, I'm touched that he still cares enough to tell me, to encourage me. And sometimes discourage me! But I'm touched just the same.

You're only fooling yourself by hiding in your comfort zone. When someone says that you're aiming too low, I'll bet most of the time they're right. And if you do step too far, don't see it as a failure.

See it as another opportunity, another experience, but take a new direction. Count the experiences. Don't count the failures. If you don't apply to a certain college because you don't think you can get in, then you missed out on an opportunity. You missed out on an experience that might have been right for you. It might have been the perfect challenge. It might have been fun. You never know.

Don't feel guilty about having high expectations. Be proud. I hate it when girls dumb themselves down. If you're the girl with all the talent, who has direction, know that others see you that way, too. If you feel good about yourself, don't apologize for that. Don't apologize for your talents and gifts.

One of my players, Katie Gielow, came in at age 18 as possibly the best athlete I ever had. But she felt she should play average. She was always afraid that she'd offend others if she played as well as she really could. She wanted to be accepted. And I think she believed it would help team harmony if everyone played at the same level. But she couldn't control herself! She'd accidentally make an incredible play, and then apologize for it. That was a huge comfort zone she was stuck in. She would never be her best and help the team to be its best until she let loose.

It was fun booting her out of that comfort zone. And then she took off. Once her performance improved, she started loving it. And she quickly found out that her teammates *wanted* her to be her best. It was clear that we all enjoyed watching her unleash her athletic ability — and take pride in it. Of course, she's an All-America player.

Sometimes we have to rely on our own motivation. I was the kid in physical education class in the seventh grade who didn't improve enough. Why? Because the teacher always geared it to the middle of the road, and I was an elite athlete. I felt like, "Hey, I'm getting cheated. This is my specialty — my passion — and I'm not getting better. And they're catching up with me!" I was 12 years old, and I already knew that was a problem. The other kids were all being helped out of their comfort zone, and I was being left in mine. Bummer. Good thing I was self-motivated.

And remember, a lot of girls are late bloomers. There's nothing wrong with that. We don't all develop at the same rate. I was sometimes fooled when a new player would walk into our volleyball program. My initial thought — not my initial words! — might be, "Oh, she'll be a contributor but not an impact player." You'd be surprised how many times I was fooled. It reminded me not to prejudge. We can't assess a person's heart and drive and competitiveness.

One year, the rankings told us that we were not the best team in the nation. Their mistake! We took that as an insult. And that pulled us out of any comfort zone we were in. We still expected to win another national title. And we did. We cranked it up. Emmy Sjogren was one of four seniors who carried us that year.

She had not been a hotshot recruit coming in. In fact, she didn't even make the travel team her rookie year. We had 14 players and we traveled with 12. She was one of the two who stayed home.

But by the time she was a senior, she was first-team All-America. She went through more comfort zones in her four years than any player I ever had. Impressive! She challenged herself well beyond the norm. I really believe that her rookie year — when she was left behind — that she knew she'd be All-America some day. She was heart-smart. She had her own agenda. She watched the older players and learned from them. She had tremendous passion. She had tremendous work ethic.

Not to mention a secret weapon that she had all along: Her wit. She was a fun player to watch, and a fun player to be around, and she made us laugh. Constantly. Our team loved to be around Emmy. My own daughters love to be around Emmy. I love to be around Emmy.

Emmy will never be left behind again. Not a chance. She's now a successful business person in Atlanta. And she just returned from helping build playgrounds for children in Vietnam.

Talk about leaving your comfort zone!

My teams always toed the line. Here they stand at attention while the opponent is introduced. (Washington University in St. Louis Photographic Services)

"Discipline in any sport or any activity enhances skill."

ATTENTION: DETAIL
(DISCIPLINE)

"If we train for surprises, they are no longer surprises."

Okay, girls: Toe the line. We're talking discipline!

I don't believe in lucky breaks. I believe in attention to detail. Some people believe discipline to be negative. Contrary to that notion, discipline is a great experience. It's not just a trip to the principal's office. Discipline encourages a pat on the back, not a paddle to the rear end.

Discipline is control, through practice and repetition, over a facet of your life. Or many facets. And discipline in any sport or any activity enhances skill. By doing the same activity hundreds of times, we learn to do it with the same style, the same emotions, the same mental edges. And we become accomplished.

When learning to serve a volleyball, it's imperative that you have a specific routine that you go through every time. When I was coaching high school volleyball, a girl named Kelly Knott was going back to serve. Many players bounce the ball before they toss it up to hit it. Before Kelly bounced it, she let out a whopper of a sneeze. And I said, "That's too bad. Now you have to sneeze every time you serve for the rest of your life." That's discipline!

You can look at any athletic team and know if they're disciplined. At Washington University, I was always proud of the way Joe ran pregame warm-up. In giving that responsibility to my assistant, it became his pregame show. And our warm-up was highly disciplined. We actually practiced that practice! Our players loved it. The fans loved it. And we absolutely sent a message to our opponents with our warm-up. They would often be watching us, sometimes mesmerized, instead of performing their own pregame routine. We were so disciplined that we could run our warm-up without a ball and still be ready to play.

In fact, once after a lackadaisical performance on the road, we came back home and practiced the next day. As the team was setting up, I calmly said, "Put the balls away. We don't need them." We had a three-hour practice of what I called "focus drills" with no volleyballs. At one point, we were doing a scrimmage-like drill with no ball, and both sides actually thought that there would be a winner!

That's how effective it was. It also showed how disciplined my players were in their approach. They sweated through two T-shirts each and were exhausted. They ended up liking it, even though they were hesitant at the start. So how did I reward them? We did it the next day, too. They readily agreed at the end of the two days that we had re-established our well-known discipline. The third day, they didn't even get the volleyballs out.

Many young athletes measure their performance for the day in the warm-up.

That's a mistake. What you do in the warm-up makes absolutely no difference in your performance during the game. *Repeat*: The warm-up makes absolutely no difference in the game. You obviously want to be attentive to detail so you truly do warm up every muscle you will use. How many homeruns Mark McGwire hits in batting practice has nothing to do with how many he hits in the game. Hey, it's a warm-up, not a measurement of success. That goes for practicing the piano or any other activity where you have to prepare yourself.

Keeping everything in the same order on your desk every day is important. If something is out of order, that's where your attention may wander, instead of on your homework. The same way with how neat you keep your backpack or your locker or your bedroom or kitchen. I know that sounds so menial, so trivial, but attention to detail is key to winning. It's the difference between a winner and a wannabe. And attention to detail is the heart of discipline. Our opponents often mimicked us, and we found copycats to be quite flattering.

If you have enough repetitions and detail work, when you get in a strange or tense moment in competition, it's less of a crisis. Everything will be familiar to you because you've practiced.

No detail is too simple or too small. When we entered a gym, our players carried their bags on their right shoulders. During a match, the bags were lined up in a perfect row. Maybe a rookie on the other team was chilled by this army of Washington University Bears. And maybe she elbowed one of her teammates and said, "Hey, look at that!"

Yes, it could be somewhat intimidating to opponents. But we did it for our own pride, our own cohesiveness. Our players knew that this made us special. We were all on the same wavelength. We were all in this together.

Little details are a big part of discipline. On our team, a lot of the traditions or disciplines were created by the players. Our team came up with a private, motivational saying every year. Each player taped a letter on the back of her shoes. When we put the letters all together in the right order, they spelled out the words of that year's theme.

One year our theme was, "It's a ring thing," because our focus was on winning that national championship ring. Another year, it was "Prepare to die," because . . . well, because. We never told anyone outside the team what the theme was. Parents and friends always tried to piece the puzzle together. They tried to figure it out. In fact, students all over campus spent an enormous amount of time trying to crack the code each year. We all had a lot of laughs. See what I mean about discipline being fun?

When we drove to matches in our vans, the rookies sat in the rear, then the sophomores, then the juniors, and then the seniors closest to the coaches, up front in the seats of honor. The rookies pumped the gas, singing the school fight song while they did it, and cleaned the van when we got back. It was a tradition, a discipline, created by the players, not me. It was not harassing or demeaning. These chores had to be done. The players did them for one year and never had to do them again. It was good clean fun.

Every year at the first team meeting, the coaches stepped out of the room, and the players developed a policy about alcohol that would stand all the season. It's an amazing challenge for young people to back away from peer pressure when it comes to drinking. My team voted on this for 13 years, and every year, every player pledged to have an alcohol-free season. I could never tell them enough how proud I was of that decision.

That's a tough task. They still went to parties. Players told me that they held cups of water so that they weren't pressured by friends. No one else needed to know what they were drinking. Before long, much of the campus realized that volleyball players didn't drink, and the other students rarely offered them alcohol, because they respected their decision. I really believe kids crave discipline. We all do.

Discipline is not always someone telling us what to do. It's a matter of *knowing* what to do ourselves, keeping in mind good morals and values.

It's also about seemingly smaller things. It's planning. It's organizing. It's time-management. We think little of wasting five minutes at practice or in our daily routines. But when you do it 10 or 20 times, it's an issue. That's critical time. I'm proud that my own children have a homework routine — snack, homework, homework in book bag, put away, do your chore, play. It's a rare exception that we break that routine. It's that important. I appreciate busy hands, busy minds, busy lives.

Our summer volleyball camps for young girls were built on discipline. And the players loved it. Shirts tucked in. Hair pulled back. Knee pads up. Hustling between drills. Quiet respect for speakers. And laughing at all of my jokes! The structure was appreciated by campers and coaches alike, because it gave us more time to play and have fun. And those little disciplines brought all of us together and helped make it *our* camp.

We were different from other camps. The campers knew they were special just by being there. It was one of the most challenging sports camps in the nation. They accepted the challenge. And our return rate each year was over 80 percent of our 1,200 campers. That proved that they thrived on the discipline. They didn't fear the demands. And it made them better players and, I know, better people.

Discipline encourages attention to detail. There's no doubt that the biggest winners in our society pay attention to the finer points of life. We hear that the rich get richer. It's true. Our team was rich, and kept getting richer, because we had such a disciplined work ethic. Great student-athletes wanted to study and play at Washington University. It wasn't by accident that we got richer. And it wasn't by luck.

When the ball rolls along the top of a volleyball net and then drops on the opponent's court, that's not luck. The player put enough spin to make the ball fall that way. We create the outcomes, big or small, by practicing attention to detail. Winners get the breaks. Actually, I don't like to call them breaks. Don't tell me I'm lucky. Tell me I'm disciplined. There are no real breaks in life. Talking about luck is fantasy talk. There is no such a thing as lucky break. We create the outcomes.

I don't believe in superstition. There are no lucky or unlucky numbers. I like having 13 chapters in this book. Wearing the same bow in your hair every game doesn't win either. It may be fun, but it doesn't win. When a player said that she wasn't washing her uniform because we won, I said, "Take it off and get it in the laundry." I'm not amused by superstitious beliefs. And what's this with rubbing a rabbit's foot? It won't get you anywhere. *You* make the difference in the outcome, not some phony fur on a chain.

And while I'm hot, there's no such thing as a lucky meal. There is such a thing as proper nutrition and the right amount of sleep. Concentrate on that. You might stick with a meal or a bedtime that gets you ready to be at your best. But that's not luck.

So that's what I mean by discipline, and why it helps us compete. Somewhere in our society, discipline gained a negative notoriety. Somewhere in our family and educational systems, discipline started to mean punishment. And we've all experienced that — having to stay in for recess or getting detention. Hey, when I was a little girl, I got a ruler across the knuckles in school for saying my name was "Teri" instead of "Therese." That must have been in the waning days of corporal punishment!

Remember, discipline is not always something done to us. It's a tool that we can use to our benefit. Make your discipline your responsibility. And I'll make my discipline mine! When I saw our players starting our traditions — our disciplines — on their own, I very much appreciated it. Winners pay attention to detail more efficiently than most people. They realize what it does for them. Little things do lead to big things.

Our volleyball team won all those titles and set all those records. But when people saw us play, their first reactions were often:

"Wow, look at how disciplined they are," and "Wow, look how much fun they're having."

Odd, isn't it. Or is it?

Kathy Bersett, 1990 national player of the year, dons the warm-up shirts we wore the year after our first national championship. (Washington University in St. Louis Photographic Services)

"Our dream was always to become national champions. And we did. A lot."

DREAM ON
(AIMING HIGH)

"I focus on the future today. I focused on today yesterday."

When my daughter Manda was four years old, she loved volleyball and always said she'd be a volleyball coach like her mom. That was her dream. She always asked to go on every volleyball trip we had at Washington University. Finally, I told her she could go with us to an off-season exhibition tournament.

Manda was so excited. She was up at 5 AM. When we got to our campus to meet the team, she said, "We're going on a bus?" It was just a 15-seat passenger van, but Manda kept saying, "We're going on a bus!" That's all she could talk about. I got behind the wheel and we drove to the tournament about two hours away. Manda got to watch me coach, and she got to hit the ball around with the players between matches, and then we got in the van to drive home.

The players started talking about what they wanted to be when they grew up. Yes, they still do that in college. Somebody asked Manda what she wanted to be. I was sitting at the wheel, all proud, because I knew she wanted to be a volleyball coach like her mom.

And then Manda said, in her most grownup voice, "I'm going to be a volleyball bus driver!"

The team cracked up. That was a reminder of how quickly our dreams can change and go in a lot of different directions.

Dreaming is healthy. It motivates us to get where we want to go, whether we're going on a bus or not. How can I ever get ahead if I'm not dreaming about tomorrow? If I'm only looking at today, I'm always playing catch-up.

Surround yourself with people who dream. If you're not getting support at home, you need to be around people who dream — because pursuing your dream can be a struggle at times. You'll need support.

Angie Suarez especially wanted to study and play volleyball with us at Washington University. She was admitted quickly because she's a bright girl. But tuition was expensive. We didn't give athletic scholarships and she didn't get the financial aid that she needed.

She called me up in tears to tell me that. I said I was sorry. But right away she said, "It's not over yet, Coach." She assured me that she was meeting the next day with the financial aid department. She did get more aid, but not much more. I told her again that I was sorry. She was still not defeated. She said, "No problem, Coach. I just met with the assistant director. Tomorrow I'm meeting with the director."

She kept after her dream, and she eventually made it happen. Angie was the most enthusiastic player I ever had. She knew what she had to do to follow her dreams. She now has a master's degree in occupational therapy and lives in Beijing, China. Every time she e-mails me, she's off on a train to a new adventure somewhere in Asia.

It's no accident that at our summer volleyball camp we put our youngest players in a group called "Dreamers." They were in first to fifth grades. One girl, Holly Ratkewicz, first came to our Dreamers when she was in third grade. She announced that she would grow up to be a Washington University Bear. So when camp ended, I wrote her a note that said, "I'll see you when you're a Bear someday."

Holly kept that note all through high school. We did recruit her, and she did become a Bear. And she lived her years at Washington University like it was her lifelong dream, which it was. She was known across campus for her humor and dedication. It was nothing for Holly, on the day of a match, to slit open an old volleyball and wear it on her head to class. She wanted everyone to know that we had a match that night.

It's easy to see why Holly was so successful in reaching her dream. She had tremendous family support at home. That's obviously a boost. If you don't have that kind of encouragement, that's where your competitive spirit aids you. You have to dream in spite of the struggles facing you. Lack of money. Lack of en-couragement. Peer pressure. Hurtful remarks from other people.

When my Manda got a little older, I remember her asking me, "Mom, do physical therapists make much money?" I told her, "Be what you want to be. And if you're the best at what you do, no matter what it is, you'll make money." You don't always need a lot of help from others when you're dreaming. My

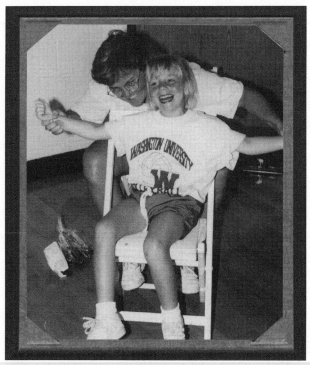

Mom and Manda at Dreamers Camp.

husband and I always encouraged our young children to cut pictures out of magazines that appeal to them. The activity sparked dreaming.

Maybe you want to be a florist, and your parents don't know enough about it to support you. You can go to a florist in town and volunteer as an intern. There's a lot to be said for volunteering or apprenticing with someone who is living your dream. That helps point you in the right direction. Or it may show you that that dream is not really right for you.

And it is healthy to change your dream. I constantly hear young children say, "Is it okay to be a coach *and* a doctor?" Or they'll say, "Can I be a lawyer *and* pick up trash?" When I was 13, I spent two years as a Candy Striper in a hospital, volunteering to help patients. Talking to them. Delivering flowers. Changing bed linens. I didn't go to medical school. That was not my dream. But the experience was invaluable in teaching me compassion.

I determined in fourth grade that my dream was to coach. That's a long time to stick with the same dream. That's not the norm, because most young people change their dreams again and again. That's not bad. That's not failure. That shows you have confidence. You're not afraid to dream, to try something else, to push out of your comfort zone. This process is a large part of the enjoyment of dreaming. Remember, winners thrive on that process. Envision the final result, but also enjoy the drive along the way.

Once, our family had just moved into a new house where the walls were still plain white. I was tucking Manda into her in bed and I said, "What are we going to do to decorate your room?" And she said, "Right above my bed, I want to paint, 'Better call me Manda now, because soon you'll be calling me Miss President!'"

She was 10 years old then. Now, at 14, she has painted clouds and stars on her walls…really conducive to dreaming.

Look at your dream as your ultimate aim. You also have short-term goals. Those mini-dreams were difficult for our volleyball team when we started winning all the time. Our dream was always to become national champions. And we did. A lot. But it was hard to make short-term goals for smaller tournaments. What were supposed to dream, "For a change, let's try to come in second this time!" No way!

So our short-term goals were mostly off-court. Always speak positively about your teammates. Sit and study together. Find ways to motivate and inspire your teammates. Put a special note or quote or poem up in the locker room. All of these smaller victories along the way help you reach your ultimate aim.

You should have lofty dreams. Amy Sullivan, one of my All-America players, dreamed of being a medical doctor. That's a pretty competitive dream. It was clear that she had the capabilities of realizing her dream. She had excellent grades, good study habits, and was committed to the task at hand. She's now a doctor at a major St. Louis hospital. I knew Amy had chosen the right path when I recently asked her, "Are you happy?" And she said, "Oh, Coach, it is *so awesome*!"

I was so happy for her. Medical school is a long grind, yet she gutted it out to achieve that dream. You also have to be brave. You have the courage to believe in yourself. Just tap into your heart. If someone is a junior in college, it takes courage to say, "Mom, Dad, guess what? I changed my major." That just might be the time that you don't get the support from your parents! Maybe it means that you have to pay for an extra year of college to take all the courses for your new major. Always remember: To gain courage, encourage yourself constantly.

A dream is not the same as a fantasy. To dream the impossible dream is not always healthy. The song should be "The *Improbable* Dream." If it's impossible, you'll be frustrated. You have to have the tools to make your dream come true. Know your strengths and weaknesses, and then adjust your dream. Allow for mistakes. You'll still move forward.

If you live in the desert and want to be a marine biologist, be realistic. Change your dream, or find a school by a large body of water. It doesn't mean you quit dreaming. It doesn't mean you aim low. It doesn't mean you set easy goals. But if you jump out of an airplane at 30,000 feet without a parachute, and your dream is to land safely, you'll be crushed.

My daughter Gabi insisted from age four to age six that she would be Snow White when she grew up. Unless she was talking about improvisation at Disney World, I don't think she'll be in the woods when she's 18, living with seven dwarfs and waiting for Prince Charming. It's okay to fantasize when you're eight. If you're still doing it at 18, you may have a problem. A fantasy involves a pretend world. A dream is something you are planning to achieve with some measurable steps along the way. Simply put, there are no easy formulas for dreaming. It's a personal thing. It may be the most personal thing we've talked about in this book. If you need one basic guide for dreaming, try this:

Follow your heart, but use your head.

"A strong self-esteem leads to self-worth. Self-worth is knowing that you're valuable — to yourself and others."

Chris Roettger demonstrates the value of a hug. (Washington University in St. Louis Photographic Services)

THE FEEL-GOOD FILE
(SELF-ESTEEM)

"I work at being humble with who I am. But I also want to be proud of who I am."

Stop the chapter. Grab a piece of paper — right now! Okay? Jot down 10 reasons why you like you. Others might not even know these things about you. Start writing. Fast! Here, I'll do it, too.

Ten things I like about me:
1. My enthusiasm
2. My love for competition.
3. I love hugs.
4. I love to have fun.
5. I love working with youth.
6. Evaluating. Everything. People, houses, decorating.
7. I absolutely crave physical activity.
8. I love to read.

9. I love being in front of a crowd. I'm a ham.

10. I love my family.

Hey, I could do 40 more, because it's fun to write good things about yourself. You can do it, too. We all have egos. We know who we are, and we know what it takes to make us happy. I hope when you do your list that you'll be laughing like I did. You've got a lot of things to like about yourself, too, don't you?

I don't have to write my faults. In fact, *do not write down your faults!* They jump out at you anyway. They'll be way too clear in your life. And if they aren't, don't worry, others will tell you. They won't always tell you what's good about you. So forget negative comments. Keep a built-in eraser in your mind. And use it.

Have you figured out this chapter yet? Self-esteem is how I feel about me. You can have strong self-esteem or weak self-esteem. Sometimes I need to note its importance in my own life — physically, emotionally, mentally, and spiritually. Sometimes I need to remind myself about that. So after you write down those 10 things you like about yourself, get a folder and put the list in there.

That will be your first entry in your Feel-Good File. Then start adding other things that make you feel good. You like a photo in a magazine? Rip it out and put it in your Feel-Good File. You bought a cool shirt that made you feel great when you wore it? Jot that down and put it in your Feel-Good File. You have a crazy photo of you and your best friend? Save it in your Feel-Good File. You could even create a journal of your thoughts. It's also a good idea to make a list of what you're grateful for.

Girls like to connect with people. So don't be afraid to share your Feel-Good File with others. My own Feel-Good File includes cards from friends, funny lines that people say, articles, programs from events, photos, and my most special treasure — the first quilt patch I ever made. I made it with my grandma when I was 10 years old, and I remember everything about that day.

As I keep adding to my file, I'll get better at feeling better about myself — just as I'll improve if I serve a volleyball 200 times, or practice my piano piece every day for a month. Then, when you have a rotten moment, open up your file. You just might need to look at one paper or one picture to cheer yourself up. Then close up the folder and put it away until you need it again.

We also have an intangible Feel-Good File in our minds. Tuck special memories and moments there. Recall them when you need pumping up. It's a confidence builder. Be responsible for your own happiness. Maintain an inventory of good times in your mind.

And don't forget the Feel-Good Files of others. It's also our responsibility to help fill the files of our family and friends. For example, we e-mail so much these days, we forget how special it can be to receive a card. Or to send a card, too.

A strong self-esteem leads to self-worth. Self-worth is knowing that you're valuable — to yourself and to others. Both self-esteem and self-worth make me a better competitor. These are two of the tools that winners use. Everyday. Many times a day. Why? When I feel good about myself, my confidence increases, and that increases my chances of winning. No doubt.

A lot of girls are too critical of themselves. And who wouldn't be? For years, others have whined about us and to us. And we sometimes whine about ourselves. We're given messages every day that there's something wrong with us. Open any magazine, and almost every page is telling us we're too fat, too short, too tall, too blonde, not blonde enough. Who cares? Hey, I'm not listing my faults — or what others think are my faults. Forget it. I want to be the best I can be. It's okay to *strive* for perfection, but how often can we actually be perfect? Never.

Suppose you had a piano recital, you messed up, and you didn't have your best performance. So what? It's one day. One performance. Maybe you did the same song perfectly 25 times with your piano teacher. It's not that you shouldn't care. You do. You're a competitor, but you're not competing with yourself. So don't beat yourself up. You're on *your* team. You're not with the opposition.

Enough other people will try to beat you down. Don't help them. Take this whole popularity game we play. We're constantly trying to figure out where we fit. If we feel good about ourselves, we'll feel comfortable with our role among others. Believe that you're important with whatever group you choose to be with. Believe that your opinion matters. Believe that you're valuable.

Of course there are cliques. There will always be cliques. No doubt, there is competition when you are with peers. It's not always spoken competition. Sometimes it's a glaring look. Strong self-esteem and self-worth help you decide where you want to be. You have the power to make good decisions. If it's time to leave your comfort zone, remember: You'll know it. If a group of peers make you uneasy, get out. Be heart-smart. It's time to move on.

Look at the title of the book. Hey, life *is* competition. I'm telling you that these competitive moments go on all day long, day after day. You have small victories moment after moment, all day long. And you don't even realize it. You got up by your alarm clock. You dressed appropriately for the weather. You planned your schedule for the day. You chose your nutrition. And you're learning not to care if others say, "You should have a red apple instead of a green apple." Don't change your mind. Don't change your apple. Don't see it as a fault. You picked it out. Obviously, *you* liked it. Stick with it.

When someone says something ugly to you, I know it pains your heart momentarily. I know it hurts. But when someone says something that makes me say "ouch," I try to say "ouch" and move on. Because I'm not dwelling on negatives, remember? Some people may cry. That's okay. I'm actually a crier myself. We all express our emotions differently. Just say "ouch" and move on. Don't dwell on it. If someone says or does something nasty to you, take a timeout and take yourself out of the game. Go to the girls' room or your locker or an empty room — or just find a friend's shoulder — and compose yourself. Say "ouch," get yourself back together and move on.

But don't retaliate. I'm not into paybacks. Because then I'm responding to the person who hurt me, instead of focusing on myself. Don't give that person the satisfaction of seeing you hurt. Why focus on a tormentor? You have good self-esteem and self-worth on your side. Hey, I still say "ouch" when I read an article in the paper critical of me. Or when I hear someone say something that hurts my heart. I still ache.

But I've learned to treasure myself. I have high self-esteem. And, don't forget, I've got my Feel-Good File to help me. I recover well from painful moments, but they still happen. Believe me, I'm 44 years old, and they happen.

My son, Will, was struggling with poor self-esteem early in ninth grade. He is a distance runner and loves the sense of freedom it provides. I still remember the day when Will came home from a four-mile run after establishing a personal best. He was so excited, which was huge because he is so introverted. I knew that he needed a very visual and very constant feel-good file.

So I said, "Will, grab my craft paints and go paint your success on your bedroom wall." I gave him no rules. I was a little concerned about what his room would look like when he got done. He had written, *On January 12th, 2000, Will T. Clemens established a new personal record in the four-mile run.* It's the first thing he sees when he wakes up. It's the last thing he sees when goes to bed.

Now, I'm not necessarily encouraging each of you to paint how great you are all over the house. But it does help to paint a pretty picture of yourself somewhere. Know that the person you're becoming is that pretty picture.

Girls have special areas of concern. Weight, in particular, can become an issue. I learned to emphasize fitness and nutrition with my players and maintain a positive approach. I didn't harp on their weight. If we dwell on our faults, bad things can happen. In this case, they can lead to anorexia. Or bulimia. Or ulcers. Or depression.

Focus on strengths. They give us more championship moments. And those moments are more widespread than we might think. Applause from an audience. A hug from a friend. An "atta girl" from a favorite teacher. Those all boost self-esteem, self-worth, and self-confidence. Those moments all show that we're winning.

And they're worth going after. Because you're worth it. And when you get those special victories, they will be very special entries in your Feel-Good File.

PICK YOUR POCKETS
(DECISION MAKING)

"God determines our talent. We choose how to use it."

What can I do now? What little girl hasn't asked that on a hot summer day? And then there are people like me who ask, "What's going to make me a better competitor?"

Imagine that you have on a coat. The entire coat is covered with pockets, which represent the choices of activities you have. And you fill them with things that are valuable to you. In essence, you put time in these pockets.

Your own experiences in life determine what to put in there. In making choices — and in competition — gathering information is key. Each pocket represents a passion. Here's what my coat looks like. I have a pocket for coaching volleyball, a pocket for professional speaking, a pocket for my conditioning, a pocket for playing golf, a pocket for my music, a pocket for my family.

Those are my biggies. I also have several smaller pockets. You pick the

Two of my players, Chris Roettger and Nikki Holton, do flood relief work the week before the NCAA Finals.

"I'm an achiever. So every day when I get up, I ask myself what I want to accomplish. I want my choices to make me feel proud and fulfilled."

passions that pack your pockets, and you pick the pockets you want to pack. Repeat that five times as fast as you can!

Okay, whether you can say that tongue-twister or not, the point is that you decide what your passions will be. There's no doubt that girls seek approval. So often, girls do what others want them to do. Hey, you do it and I do it. Girls need to be strong girls. Women need to be strong women. People need to be strong people. It goes back to declaring your independence.

So how do we make choices? A good society, a healthy society demands that we make choices on our needs and the needs of others. Just like a team. There aren't any special steps to making a decision, really. Try to find something that is challenging, makes you compete harder and have fun.

I'm an achiever. So every day when I get up, I ask myself what I can accomplish. I want my choices to make me feel proud and fulfilled. There's a purpose behind my choices. As a competitor, I do not randomly decide what to do. I focus on my basic needs: Social, mental, physical, spiritual, and emotional.

Let's say that right now, I'm feeling a physical and a social need. So I open my conditioning pocket and decide to ride bikes with a friend. Does that sound simple? It is.

Remember, girls like to connect with others. There's a part of me that loves to compete *with* people, and not just compete *against* people. So when I'm riding bikes with my friend, I don't always race against her. We might challenge a steep hill together, and help push each other to the top. We're competing against the hill, not each other. Just like a team, we worked together, yet still filled our individual needs.

Some choices are givens and some are not. A competitor makes an automatic choice to study for a chemistry test. If you have a test the next day, you do it. And some choices are obviously more important than others.

Daily decision-making can be something as simple as, "I'm going to the movies. What's everybody going to wear? Is it important that I ask them, or can I make my own decision?" For some people, that's highly competitive. Peer pressure can be grueling. Been there, done that.

Different people put different values on these choices. Some people put social decisions on a high level. For me, physical growth is a high priority each day. I need to move. We need to base our decisions on our needs. It all comes down to experiences. Older people have more experiences. That doesn't mean young girls can't make good decisions. Oftentimes older people — parents, coaches, teachers — can help young girls because of their broader experiences.

We can choose to fill our pockets any way we want. We can fill 20 pockets half full, or five pockets most of the way, or overload one pocket till it's bursting at the seam. But what will happen if I fill one pocket as full as I can get it, and the others are empty? People who want to excel at the top level of any activity, such as making the Olympic team, must put an extreme amount of time into one pocket. That can leave little time to put in other pockets.

Our championship program at Washington University demanded that our players put a lot of time into their volleyball pocket. They had a priority system. While their social pocket was sometimes short-changed, their academic pocket was not.

Sometimes when we're young, parents make some decisions for us. They may also steer us toward a new activity. They may tell us how much we will put into our study pocket or our chores pocket. They may limit us on the amount of time we put into our social pocket. Hey, parents have been around the block. While we don't always agree, they sometimes have to make the calls. My own parents required that I do an hour of chores every day after school. My best friends didn't do as much at their homes. While that ticked me off then, I grew to be organized and to have a strong work ethic. Wonder where I got that?

Specializing is good. It can be good at age five and age 12 and age 20, but not at the risk of emptying all your other pockets. Remember, my volleyball players specialized, yet did not neglect all other pockets. Along with their academic load, I encouraged them to be involved in campus activities and family events. Their freedom to be in other activities gave them a fresh approach to volleyball. I'm convinced we would not have won all those championships had they been one-dimensional.

There are unhealthy choices, too. You can fill one pocket too full. If you get one pocket overloaded, start unzipping! Start putting time in another pocket. Each girl has to decide what is good, and what is better, for her. Make sure you're happy. And know if it's time for a change.

I know a girl, Katie, who home-schooled for four years so she could concentrate on figure skating. That was the activity she loved most in life. She even moved away from home for two years to get better coaching. Then, right before her senior year of high school, she called her mom. Katie said she was tired of skating and wanted to come home and go to high school for her last year with her younger sister. She just wanted to be a *normal* kid again.

Katie had filled her pocket quite full with skating. She wanted to start filling other needs — emotional, mental, and social. Obviously, she had a lot of confidence to make such a huge change in her life. She had a great support system with her family. And she felt comfortable enough to say, "Okay, that's enough. I'm finished with that pocket." She may not want anything to do with skating now, but she can always go back to that pocket later. Even if she doesn't, look what that pocket gave her. Self-confidence. Self-discipline. Self-esteem. Self-worth.

Katie made that decision by herself. You may decide to go to a friend, a parent, a sister, or a teacher for advice. It's a good healthy thing to do. You're a good, strong girl, but maybe you didn't have enough experiences to make a wise decision. Go to a person who has more pockets filled.

It's also inviting to peek into someone else's pockets. You're looking for ideas. Girls who are looking for direction should look to other girls. Girls ask girls. I really believe that. It doesn't mean that you can't ask guys. But girls understand girls. It's healthy for a father to help his daughter find female role models. I'm encouraging female leaders and role models to mentor girls.

My 14-year-old, Manda, enjoys showing me what's in her pockets. Sometimes I have no clue what's coming. The other day, she sprung on me that she wants to be a pediatric physical therapist. She was anxious to show that pocket to me. So I had her spend a day with a physical therapist. She loved it.

The pockets you pick define who you are. So pick those pockets and pack them passionately.

11

GET UP AND GO
(MOTIVATION)

"We'd leave our national championship trophy up for one day. Then we'd put it away and start thinking about the next one."

We all know that there is an energy crisis in the world today. We as competitors sometimes suffer from the same crisis. We all find it's hard to get our motors running some days. If we're striving to be more competitive and to achieve at a higher level, motivation might be the most important fuel we need.

Motivation includes both encouragement and influence. Some of us don't need to be motivated by anybody but ourselves. Self-motivated girls encourage themselves to move forward. Others need constant nudging.

We talked earlier about staying within our personalities while competing. It's awesome when one of the personalities on a team is high-spirited and inspirational. Kathy Bersett was the spirit of our sport at Washington University. After my first year there as volleyball coach, we had some high-powered talent, but we needed to add a sparkplug like Kathy. I had coached her for two years in high

" Motivation encourages high energy. When someone pumps you up, your adrenaline flows at a greater rate. And that inspires you to get up and go!"

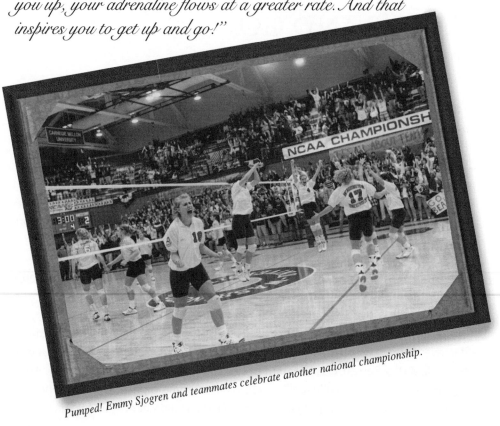

Pumped! Emmy Sjogren and teammates celebrate another national championship.

school, so she knew my fast-paced, intense style of play. And I knew that she was the catalyst that we needed.

Her scrappy, sweaty, pat-on-the-back, coming-at-ya, in-your-face, bring-it-on style of play did exactly what I hoped it would. She was relentless. She would not let anyone slow the pace of our practices, not even me. Opponents were astounded by our newfound intensity. She helped lift us to our first national championship. And by her senior year, she was named the national player of the year.

Motivation encourages high energy. When someone pumps you up, your adrenaline flows at a greater rate. And that inspires you to get up and go! Our teams used the buddy system. At the beginning of each season, I threw the names of everyone — players and coaches — into a cup. We each drew out one secret buddy to motivate that year.

It was our charge to inspire that person with creative strategies. It could be a note, quote, or poem on your locker. It could be a water gun before our next match that might say, "Spray the Titans." It could be a stuffed eagle, the other team's mascot, hanging by the neck on your locker. You might get a piece of gum with a note that said, "Chew 'em up!"

Much of the fun was trying to figure out who was sending the special inspiration your way. I never did figure out my secret buddy. I was horrible. I was 0-for-14 in guessing. To this day, I think they all plotted against me! And loved it. You could have secret buddies with your friends, too. It doesn't have to be with teammates.

Every girl does not constantly need a pat on the back or a kick in the butt to get going. I know I'm self-motivated, and I'm told it's contagious. The truth is, I'm inspired by *any* competitive opportunity. Bring it on! I can't wait! Hey, just waking up in the morning energizes me. I like to read and study how other leaders motivate. I take pride in encouraging young people, not discouraging them.

When you're discouraged or de-motivated, you become a bump on a log. Clearly, if you're reading this book, you're no bump. You're looking for ways to move forward. I'm intrinsically motivated, and this is not something mysterious. Think back to when you were a little kid playing hopscotch. If you successfully threw the rock on number six, you couldn't wait to throw it on seven. You got excited. You accomplished something. You wanted to keep going. You didn't need anyone to pat you on the back.

Some competitors think that they can't be happy until they reach the end result. I'm telling you, that's not the way it is. Back to the hopscotch game. If your ultimate goal is to win by putting the rock on 10, you should still be energized when you put the rock on six, and even more when it lands on seven. Enjoy the smaller successes. They will motivate us — if we let them.

When you go to bed, visualize your accomplishments from that day. Maybe you finished a book report in English. And helped your little sister load the dishwasher. And rode bikes four miles with a friend. Be proud of what you accomplished that day. And recognize that you were motivated.

Some days, it's not easy. We all have that feeling at times. You might sit in front of the TV and feel so unmotivated. You don't want to go jogging. You don't want to make your bed. Your don't even want to call a friend.

What can you do to get going? Change directions. Look at the positive. What good will come from jogging? Maybe it's to be in better shape. Or to keep up with my teammates at practice. Or to see the wild flowers in that field two miles down the road.

If you drill yourself that way, and continue to think positively, it will become a habit. Motivation is an attitude. Sometimes people like to say, "Hey, you have an attitude." On my team, that's a compliment. Because our attitude is a positive one. Optimists achieve more because they believe they can improve. Pessimistic girls would not make it on my team. I would not recruit them. I would never surround myself with negative people, no matter how talented they are.

Optimism is contagious. Unfortunately, so is pessimism. Both can infect others, too. If my friend tells me that she has the flu, a pessimist says, "Oh, great, now I'll catch it from her." An optimist says, "Is there anything I can do to make you feel better?"

Do this experiment. Go through a day and mentally count the positive comments you make. And put a rubber band on your wrist and snap it every time you make a negative comment. If you have a bruised wrist, you need an attitude adjustment. Again, you're developing. And the habit is a positive one. And painless.

I have a friend, Candace Martz, who calls me regularly and says, "Happy day! Just happy day!" It makes me feel good. It motivates me. And I always laugh. I like to make up notes of inspiration to myself and stick them around my room. Here's a nice gift for a family member or friend who is struggling: Get one of those sticky notepads and write something inspirational on every page for them. The message could be a touching comment or an inside joke or a goofy drawing. You've given of your time, which is more motivating than being materialistic.

When I determined I had to quit coaching because of my health, I was really sad. My daughter Carly was eight years old then. She drew me a picture and wrote, "I love you mom. You are my coach." Except she spelled it *coch*. Even an eight-year-old could figure out how much I was aching inside. I was so touched. She and I laminated that message on a wooden tray, which sits in my room. I also saved the original paper and put it in my Feel-Good file. I still think, "Wow! I was inspired by my eight-year-old to be a better parent."

Notice that we're not defining a motivator by age or position. No matter what kind of team we're on, we can all help each other get up and go. I do that just by telling a friend, "You look great today!" You don't need a coach with a whistle or a teacher with a ruler. Accept that it's your responsibility to get motivated.

If you don't feel self-motivated, surround yourself with people who are. Be innovative. If you're bored, if you don't know what to do, get with a friend who always has an idea. Then maybe that will inspire you to chip in with your own suggestions. One of my players who did just that — and more — was KC Killip. She might e-mail the entire team at 9 AM and list all the things she'd already done that day: "Ran three miles. Visited a sick friend. Did two art projects. Went to an amazing design class." She just jumped on the Internet and motivated all of us. And made us laugh.

When Katie Gielow came into our program, she was a great basketball player, a great golfer, a great all-around athlete. She could have gotten an athletic scholarship to any number of schools in other sports. But she chose to come to Washington University and play volleyball. It was her least-polished sport. But Katie said, "It's the sport I want to play, and I know I can learn it." Her attitude motivated me as a coach.

So if you're not self-motivated, find someone who is committed to the same dream. Maybe you want to eat more nutritiously. Or study biology together. Or do a service project together. We're all motivated in different ways to do different things. Sometimes all it takes to get us going is a smile or a wink or a nod. Remember the joy that comes from simple things.

Compliments are also great motivators. And say thank-you when someone praises you. That will re-motivate them to do it again. The circle never ends. And don't blow it by not accepting the praise.

Don't claim, "I could have done better," or "It wasn't that big a deal." It *is* a big deal. Everybody comes out a winner. That's how we solve the energy crisis.

"Fun is so simple."

As simple as two dozen cannisters of Silly String that I bought for just such a special occasion — our first national championship celebration.

FUN, FUN, FUN!
(HUMOR IS A MUST)

"The great mystery of our program was: Did we win because we had fun, or did we have fun because we won?"

A week after I left coaching, I was talking to Joe Worlund, my longtime assistant. I told him that my biggest fear was that I will no longer laugh till I cry. I knew that's what I would miss the most. I never thought I'd laugh again as hysterically as I did with my team. Every day for 14 years, we laughed till we almost peed in our pants. For lack of sophistication, that's just how it was.

Recently, I was having a stare-down game at home with my three youngest daughters. Carly and I were going head-to-head to see who could make the other one smile first. She made a face that just completely cracked me up. Carly said, "Mom, you're crying!" My kids hadn't seen that before. I said, "That's what I do when I laugh my best laugh."

And I ran to the computer to e-mail Joe: "I just laughed till I cried!" I was so excited. There is life after sports after all.

Why was fun so built into our volleyball program? After all, it is a game. People perform better when they're relaxed and under control. Humor helps. What we do every day should be fun. That's the game of life. Enjoy what you do. Do what you enjoy. Let your personality come through. Admittedly, I'm an instigator. Always have been. Always will be. I love to play practical jokes.

The most important thing was to have fun while we were competing. There can't possibly have been anybody in our program who didn't have fun. The stories are endless. Here are just a few.

****

My first year of coaching volleyball at Washington University, I was also assisting the women's basketball team. Both the men's and women's teams were in Boston. About nine staff members were in a van, going back to the hotel after dinner. John Schael, the athletic director, appointed me the chauffeur. Of course, nobody bothered to get me directions, and the traffic was horrible. In that area, you wander into about five states in 15 minutes if you take a wrong turn. I was so lost, so fast, and my passengers had schemed in advance to be no help at all. Mark Edwards, our 6-foot-8 men's basketball coach, was sitting in the back. He kept banging his fists on the metal ceiling, as if I'd crashed into something.

I was trying to find our hotel, which was near Harvard University. So after we drove through about our fourth state, I decided to stop and ask this man at a toll booth, "How do you get to Harvard?" And he pondered for a moment and then said, "Study!"

Everyone in the van just laughed until they rolled. It was a great rookie initiation. Fun was going to be a big part of my career, even during a disaster.

* *

Once we were ranked No.1 in the nation. In two days, we were to play the No. 2 team, the University of California-San Diego. It was our biggest match of the year so far. My team wasn't responding in practice, so halfway through I said, "Every one of you hit the showers, put on a new set of practice clothes and get back up here."

One of the captains said, "Coach, do you really want us to take a shower in the middle of practice?" I snapped, "Yes. I want every one of you back here with wet hair and new clothes."

I found out later my players had gone down and just splashed water on their hair in the sink before they changed clothes. I figured they wouldn't really shower, but I wanted them to start fresh. Instead of yelling at them, I wanted to lighten them up. They were too tense about a big game. Very seldom does anger prove a point with a team. This team came back up from the locker room, with wet hair, and started laughing. We had a great practice. And we went on to win that big match.

* *

I often broke in new players or staff members with a prank. The hot dog joke was one of my favorites.

We were on the road in the middle of our 59-match winning streak. We had a rookie sports information assistant, Kevin Bergquist. He knew I'd been hospitalized with an infection. Before the match, Kevin asked me how I felt. I said, "I feel fine now. But my doctor told me that when I start to feel poorly, I need to eat certain foods right away and I'll be fine."

The match started, and we were at a real tense moment in Game 2. Suddenly I said, "Kevin, can you run down and get me a hot dog? Right now! *Please!*" He turned white in panic and screamed, "I'm going right now! What do you want on it?" And I yelled, "Mustard and relish!" And he ran out of the gym and into the lobby to get it.

He thought he was saving me from a health crisis. He ran back from the refreshment stand, huffing and puffing and handing this hot dog to me at the bench — while this close game was still going on.

I buried my head in my hands and laughed so hard that I cried. I had no intention of taking that hot dog. So one of my assistants, Brent Ruoff, calmly said, "Here, I'll eat it." And he did, right there on the bench. And my players ate up the moment. Oh, by the way, we won the match.

* *

Clearly, you don't have to play fair to have fun. In fact, pranks sometimes invite cheating.

Once we were at our hotel on the road. Three underclassmen were sharing a room: Jackie Foley, Katie Gielow, and Dre' Richards.

I was in my room watching TV. Katie and Jackie knocked on my door to ask me a question. I said, "Hey, come on in and watch 'The Dating Game'." I was always stirring up little competitions with my players, so I said, "Let's vote on which contestant gets picked for the dates. Whoever guesses wrong has to do 20 pushups each round."

They jumped at it. They were certain the coach would be doing a "face plant" on the carpet, trying to do pushups.

What they didn't know was that this show was a repeat that I'd seen that morning. The first round, I yelled, "I think it's Bachelor Number Two!" Katie took Number One and Jackie took Number Three. So I celebrated three victories in three rounds, and they did 60 pushups apiece. I finally made a full confession. They weren't bitter. They're competitors. They just got beat unfair and square.

Just then, Dre' knocked at the door with a question. I told Jackie and Katie, "Hide!" They ducked under the beds, and I opened the door. In my best stern voice and straight face, I asked Dre', "Where are your roommates?"

She said, "That's what I wanted to ask you."

I promptly went into a long rambling lecture, noting that it was her responsibility to know the whereabouts of her roommates. Dre' was paling in fear.

Just then Katie and Jackie popped up and yelled, "Gotcha!" Involving them in Part Two of Prank Night took some of the sting out of their sore shoulders.

What a successful night for the coach. Three victims in 30 minutes. And it was all spontaneous.

* *

Many of these stories have been passed down for over a decade. And sometimes the joke was on me.

Once, we were winning easily at New York University. Joanie Subar was an All-America player, great at hitting and blocking, but she had rigid hands. She could not set the ball, and we teased her endlessly.

On one play, she set it horribly. We got the point anyway, and NYU called timeout. Before I sent my team back out on the court, I said, "Nice hands, Stiffie." The team cracked up. Anne Quenette, a rookie, had just taken a big drink from a water bottle. She was standing directly in front of me in the huddle. When she started laughing at "Stiffie," she accidentally sprayed her mouthful of water all over my face. Water was dripping off hair, nose, and chin.

The team couldn't believe that this rookie would spit all over the coach. I didn't say a word. I just glared, which thrust the team into silent hysterics. Their shoulders were shaking up and down, but they were trying to stifle their laughter.

We went out to eat that night at a laid-back diner. And I quietly connived with the waitress to play a water trick on Anne. The waitress took a pitcher and started to fill Anne's glass — and kept pouring and pouring and pouring and pouring. The water spilled onto the table, off the table, all over Anne's lap. She was soaked.

The team went berserk. And Anne didn't have to ask. She knew that the prank had come straight from the top.

* *

Then there was The Pumpkin Man. It was my fourth year as coach, two days before Halloween, and we were on the road. Lori Nishikawa, my setter, came into my hotel room to ask me a question. We had left the door open. Suddenly, this man about 50 years old just walked in.

He was wearing green leotards and an orange pumpkin suit. And he was holding a pair of scissors in his hand, as though he wanted to stab something. Or someone.

I nervously said, "What do you need?" He said, "Nothing. I'm just looking around." And he left. When I told the team about it, they all said, "Right, Coach. The Pumpkin Man?"

Two days later, we had finished the tournament and were to leave the next morning. I placed a wakeup call for my room and went to bed. When the phone rang, I jumped up, showered, dressed, and headed down to the lobby to check us all out.

When I passed a room of vending machines, there he was! The Pumpkin Man! Still dressed up! I was terrified. Honestly terrified. I ran to the front desk, got myself together, and told the clerk I wanted to check out.

She said, "Are you sure? It's only 3 AM."

I went into sheer panic. I thought, "Oh my gosh! It was the Pumpkin Man who called me!" So I picked up the lobby phone and called my assistant coach, who was asleep in his room. I was hysterical. I said, "Joe, the Pumpkin Man's in the vending room! I think he's after me!"

Joe said, "It's 3 AM. What do you want me to do?"

I said, "I want to go back to my room. Come and meet me so the Pumpkin Man doesn't get me."

Well, I got back to my hall and there's Joe, peeking out of his door across

from my room. He had not even come out to save me. He was totally uncon-
cerned, even though I was sure I was about to be stabbed by the Pumpkin Man.

So then I was scared and mad. I went into my room, locked the door and
immediately the phone rang again. It was Joe. He said, "I was just thinking, if
the Pumpkin Man has a key, he's probably in your *room*!"

At that, I screamed. I totally lost it. And then he said, "Gotcha!" So every
Halloween after that, the team felt obliged to scare me with some pumpkin caper.

I got letters from the Pumpkin Man. I found notes from him in my briefcase
and on my clipboard. An inflatable Pumpkin Man was hanging in my hotel room.
A real pumpkin, with scissors stuck into it, was floating in my hotel toilet.

Once at the conference championship, a dummy stuffed into a pumpkin
suit, with a pumpkin for a head, sat in the stands where I couldn't miss him. Even
the team's parents got in on it. They sat in the stands with pumpkin masks on.

Once I took a trip to Ohio without the team just before Halloween. I checked
into my room, and there was a sign on the window: *The Pumpkin Man is coming!* I still don't know who put that there.

I think the players really tried to outdo themselves. It became a team tradition. Every year, the players got together and told the Pumpkin Man story to
the rookies.

* *

What's the point? Just that humor helps tighten cohesiveness. And tradition makes it special. Our practices were a combination of intense work and hysterical laughter. The humor bound us together, team after team, year after year.

Ten years from now, how many of my players will be able to describe an Option 2 blocking scheme? Not many. But I bet 100 percent of them could recite the Pumpkin Man story.

Fun memories. They keep us together with the people we love. Forever. Fun is so simple. Fun. I love that word.

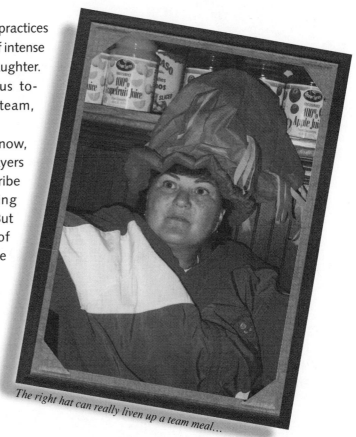

The right hat can really liven up a team meal...

GIRLS WHO GOT WITH IT
(THE LAST WORD)

"My players chose to compete, trusted my vision, and never looked back."

My favorite line from any movie is when the Good Witch in *The Wizard of Oz* tells Dorothy, "You've always *had* the power."

That's what I want each of you to remember: The power is within you!

Believe that you can capture your dream. Be passionate. Be heart-smart. Take risks. Laugh.

I know you can compete like winners because I watched girls do it every day at Washington University. My players lived this book. They lived it and loved it. Enough from me. Here it is, straight from my players' hearts!

* *

"When I first came to play for Coach Clemens, I was really passive compared to what I am now. She has made the biggest impression on my life with the confidence she's given me. I don't know what I'd be doing now if I hadn't played for her."

Amy Albers, Class of '95

Sharing a laugh with Amy Albers (Washington University in St. Louis Photographic Services)

"When we won our first national championship, it felt like we won the world."
Kathy Bersett, Class of '91

"In August 1989, when I first walked into Francis Gym, I could never have imagined I would walk away so wealthy a woman. Coach had the most incredible recipe for success. I am just beginning to understand how it worked."
Lisa Becker, Class of '93

"Coach helped me to look beyond my insecurities. Her strength of mind, body and soul is something I attempt to model every day. She helped me establish a work ethic beyond any I had known and to believe in myself — beyond my wildest dreams."
Jenny Cafazza, Class of '99

"Being competitive, to me, is the drive to succeed. And if you didn't come into the program with that drive, you sure left with it! Coach's competitiveness transferred to the team. We could feel it. It motivated us. I love competition, and I love to win."
Leslie Catlin, Class of '94

"If there is a woman who has shown me that there are no limitations to what you can do in life, it was Coach."
Melinda Doomey, Class of '01

"I often find myself thinking, 'How would Coach handle this?' Or, 'What would Coach do in this situation?'"
Kerry Fagan, Class of '90

Jess Grider, one of my "dreammakers."

"I like to think of Coach as a little ball of fire that can heat up and intensify any situation. There was never a dull moment with her around. Her powers to motivate and enliven players are like none that I have ever witnessed before and will probably never see again."

Jackie Foley, Class of '01

"I will not remember everything Coach taught me about volleyball. But I can guarantee that I will remember everything she taught me about being a strong woman and role model."

Katie Gielow, Class of '01

"Coach's tough love and tender loving care brought out the best in me. We didn't feel pressure. It was *when* we win, not *if* we win."

Nikki Gitlin, Class of '96

"Coach is a dream giver. I thank her for me. And I thank her for all the girls who now say, 'If Lovey Grider can do it, so can I!'"

Jess Lovey Grider, Class of '98

"Coach's love is a rock. She is my mentor and my friend."

Steph Habif, Class of '97

"I'm stronger, wiser, friendlier, more flexible, more easy going, more 'together.' Oh, and funnier, too! And I have Coach to thank."

Nicki Hagan, Class of '95

"The main ingredient for success is belief. And she believed in all of us."

Megan Harrod, Class of '02

"The lessons and experiences I shared with Coach will last a lifetime. I thank her for making it fun and possible."

Nikki Holton, Class of '97

"It is overwhelming to think of all the lives that Coach touched in such a special way. I thank God that I am part of her 'family.'"

Brooke Hortin, Class of '90

"We tried to prepare ourselves so there wouldn't be any surprises. We were confident that we'd be in control of things."

Liz Jokerst, Class of '95

"Coach challenged me to take my life in my own hands. For what I want to achieve, no one can take away my drive, my passion or my desire. She challenged me to find out who I am and where I'm going."

Brielle Killip, Class of '00

Michelle "Meesh" Kirwan (left) and Amy Sullivan do their farewell dance on the court before entering medical school. (Washington University in St. Louis Photographic Services)

Christine Masel, signing on as a role model. (Washington University in St. Louis Photographic Services)

"We never doubted victory. We savored everything."

Michelle Kirwan, Class of '93

"To me, laughter equated success. I thank her for giving me so many things to smile about. I know that I will cherish the laughter the most."

Jennifer Martz, Class of '99

"Coach helped me grow and mature into the person I am. She helped prepare me for the rest of my life. She taught me to be a winner, and that translates into every area of my life. I am so proud to have been her student. It is part of my identity and part of my confidence. "

Christine Masel, Class of '94

"I want to thank Coach for the preparation. The lessons learned on the court apply so well in the real world."

Kelley Meier, Class of '92

"It still amazes me how Coach could capture the attention of a room with her presence and keep everyone hanging on her every word."

Katie Michalski, Class of '02

"Our competitiveness is what set us apart from other teams, a trait we somehow inherited from our coach. We might not have been the tallest or the strongest players, but we got along well and worked our butts off. We all loved it."

Lori Nishikawa, Class of '90

That's 5' 2" Lori Nishikawa standing tall as our first national player of the year. (Washington University in St. Louis Photographic Services)

"We will always remember how thankful we are that we made it together."
Carly Price, Class of '00

"I loved the feeling that everyone wanted to beat us. It was a great feeling, actually. It meant everyone was going to play their hardest against us. And that's what made us play our best."
Anne Quenette, Class of '95

"Coach taught me lessons that could only be learned through extraordinary experiences. She inspired me more than words can say."
**Holly Ratkewicz,
Class of '00**

"Coach has proven that heart is the only true drive in competition. Not just competition on the court, but in the real world."
Andrea Richards, Class of '01

"Practice was recess. We were playing with our friends. It was intense and a reason to forget any troubles."

Chris Roettger, Class of '97

"Chapter Six, The Comfort Zone, is *my* chapter. The real memories of this team rest in the people who have been a part of it. And Coach is the glue that binds us all together."

Emmy Sjogren, Class of '97

"I hope Coach doesn't mind if I model myself after her."

Jami Struble, Class of '99

"When I take on something now, a lot more seems possible: How I deal with people, my confidence, many things that seemed like too much work. Basically, I've learned to go after what's important with everything I've got."

Angela Suarez, Class of '94

"Coach's go-for-it attitude made a lasting impression on me. What a joy it was to hear her say: 'Don't worry about mistakes, just play hard.' I noticed that if I stopped concentrating on *not* making mistakes, I made fewer."

Joanie Subar, Class of '92

"In the games when I couldn't seem to do a single thing right, a simple chat or look from Coach always motivated me."

Julie Suellentrop, Class of '02

Going cheek to cheek with Joanie Subar (above) and Julie Suellentrop (Washington University in St. Louis Photographic Services)

"Coach had a really good balance between pushing and making it fun. I learned so much from playing in the program. It was healthy competition. She taught by example that being honest is important, and that sometimes you need to let others help take care of you to make it through. I can't imagine my life without having played for her."

Amy Sullivan, Class of '94

"Competition was our life. Now it is my life."

Shelley Swan, Class of '96

"Coach gave us the chance to succeed and demanded our best. Every day."

Diane Vandegrift, Class of '90

"Coach is contagious. Nothing can hold back her intensity and devotion to all that she does. That's the reason so many people put their faith in her."

Mia Viola, Class of 02

"What always amazed me about Coach was that she always seemed to know what to say or do to pump us up. Her competitiveness was extremely catchy. No questions asked, winning is a way of life for her."

Meg Vitter, Class of '99

"Coach always said that we would treasure our memories. She was right. But she forgot to highlight the most important memory: Our coach."

Karen Wise, Class of '90

"You didn't say *I can't hack it* around Coach. You hacked it."

Claire Zellers, Class of '98

Shelley Swan, now competing in the world of finance.

Meg Vitter, whose affection for teammates was infectious.

Stayin' loose in the locker room, just before the NCAA finals. Lisa Becker, Angie Suarez, and Leslie Catlin (left to right). (Washington University in St. Louis Photographic Services)

On the bench with Joe Worlund, my sidekick for 12 years. (Washington University in St. Louis Photographic Services)

(Washington University in St. Louis Photographic Services)

About the Authors

TERI CLEMENS

In 14 years at Washington University in St. Louis, Coach Teri Clemens won seven NCAA III national volleyball championships. She was named the NCAA III national coach of the year six times and was the USA Volleyball Coach of the Year in 1997. She coached 19 different All-America players, seven national players of the year, and two players chosen as Division III All-Sports Female Athlete of the Year. Teri's players also excelled in the classroom. Five were named to the Academic All-America team and two were chosen as Academic All-America of the Year.

Teri, a graduate of and Hall-of-Famer at Truman State University, has coached in two Olympic Festivals, and speaks on motivation and competition all across America. She and Tom Clemens, both lifelong residents of St. Louis, have been married for 20 years and have adopted six children: Terri Renee, Will, Eliott, Manda, Carly, and Gabrielle.

TOM WHEATLEY

Tom Wheatley, a graduate of Bucknell University and four-time Missouri Sportswriter of the Year, writes for the *St. Louis Post-Dispatch*. He met his wife Suzanne when both were Marine Corps lieutenants. Married for 24 years, they have three children: Tom, Katie, and Carrie.